PIES

ARE AWESOME

PIES
ARE AWESOME

the definitive pie art book
STEP-BY-STEP DESIGNS FOR EVERY OCCASION

JESSICA LEIGH CLARK-BOJIN

FOREWORD BY DUFF GOLDMAN

ROCK
POINT

Brimming with creative inspiration, how-to projects, and useful information to enrich your everyday life, Quarto Knows is a favorite destination for those pursuing their interests and passions. Visit our site and dig deeper with our books into your area of interest: Quarto Creates, Quarto Cooks, Quarto Homes, Quarto Lives, Quarto Drives, Quarto Explores, Quarto Gifts, or Quarto Kids.

First published in 2021 by Rock Point, an imprint of The Quarto Group,
142 West 36th Street, 4th Floor, New York, NY 10018, USA
T (212) 779-4972 F (212) 779-6058 www.QuartoKnows.com

Rock Point titles are also available at discount for retail, wholesale, promotional and bulk purchase. For details, contact the Special Sales Manager by email at specialsales@quarto.com or by mail at The Quarto Group, Attn: Special Sales Manager, 100 Cummings Center Suite, 265D, Beverly, MA 01915, USA.

10 9 8 7 6 5 4 3 2 1

ISBN: 978-1-63106-790-7

Library of Congress Control Number: 2021941031

Publisher: Rage Kindelsperger
Creative Director: Laura Drew
Managing Editor: Cara Donaldson
Senior Editor: Erin Canning
Cover and Interior Design: Amy Sly
Layout Design: Kim Winscher

Printed in China

Safety Message

Ovens are hot. Knives are sharp. Spoiled food can make you sick. Please don't burn, stab, or poison yourself while creating your Pie Art. Okay, cool . . . now let's make some awesome stuff together!

This book is dedicated to Nis and Cillian . . .

. . . and to you, the bold Pie-oneer holding this book. I cannot wait to see all the awesome pies that you are about to bring to life and welcome you to the wonderful, creative, experimental, kooky, fun-loving, nerdy, and supportive global community of Pie Artists!

Contents

Foreword by Duff Goldman 8

Introduction 10

PART 1

The Magic of Pie Art
(Techniques)

The Pie Art Learning Curve 16

Choosing the Right Pie Dough for You 17

The Dough Test 22

Selecting Fillings, Moisture Barriers, Washes, Garnishes, and Edible Adhesives 25

Pie Art Trends 29

Supplies 32

Setting Up Your Workspace 35

Rolling Out and Handling Pie Dough 37

Cutting Pie Dough 41

Coloring Pie Dough 44

Working with Paper Templates 48

Sculpting Pie Dough 50

Working with Cutters, Plunger Cutters, and Found Objects .52

Working with Molds and Impression Mats 54

Working with Stencils 57

Trim Design 60

Putting It All Together 63

Taking Your Pies Higher 66

Displaying Your Pie Art 69

Troubleshooting 71

Planning Your Pie Art Designs and Finding Inspiration .75

PART 2

Making Memories
(Projects)

Lantern Festival Pie (Lunar New Year) 81

Tic-Tac-Toe Pie (Valentine's Day) 85

Pi Pie (Pi Day) 89

Leprechaun Hat Pie (St. Patrick's Day) 92

Bunny Pie (Easter) 99

Folk Art Bee Pie (Earth Day) 104

Quilt Pie (Mother's Day) 111

Shirt and Tie Pie (Father's Day) 116

Stars and Stripes Pie (Fourth of July) 121

Paris Skyline Pie (Bastille Day) 124

Mandala Pie (Diwali) 131

Chibi Pumpkin Pie (Halloween) 136

Monster Mouth Pie (Halloween) 141

La Catrina Pie (Day of the Dead) 144

Goofy Turkey Pie (Thanksgiving) 151

Harvest Tree Pie (Thanksgiving) 154

Snowman Pie (Winter Holidays). 159

Gelt Pie (Hanukkah) .164

Sugar Plum Fairy Pie Doll (Christmas) 169

Santa Claus Pie (Christmas) 176

Clock Pie (New Year's Eve) 183

Flying Unicorn Pie (Birthday) 186

PieKabobs (Birthday) 191

Mama and Baby Bear Pies
(Baby Shower) 194

Piescraper (Wedding) 199

Templates 206

Pie Dough and Filling Recipes 210

Preparing Your Base Pie 226

Resources 228

The Pie Art Family 230

Index 233

Acknowledgments 238

About Jessica 240

Foreword by Duff Goldman

The first time I stuck a motor in a cake two things happened. One, it didn't work. Two, everyone laughed at me.

This was back when the words *special effects* and *cake decorating* didn't coexist in the same conversation. People were sculpting cakes, but being somewhat of a tinkerer, I just wasn't thinking like a cake decorator. Now people are using 3-D printers in cakes and making them levitate and talk and move and stuff. For me, the breadth of human creativity is truly why I think we were put on this earth. When we can take two concepts, like cake decorating and electrical engineering, and bring them together, each with its own history and tradition of craft, and then in turn make something new that didn't exist before, except in the imagination, I feel that we have honestly fulfilled our purpose. Not to get too philosophical about it, but how else can we justify our frivolity?

Pies can be complex. I think about pies a lot more than you would think a cake decorator should think about pies. I like to use pies when I'm explaining baking as a concept. When I see a pie as a whole, I see a series of simple steps executed in an exact order under specific conditions that when done correctly result in a well-crafted pie. It's a nice metaphor for really anything in life. If you have never made a pie, it can seem like an incredibly daunting task. A woven-dough lattice top. A dairy-based custard that needs to be refrigerated inside a crust that is baked golden brown. What manner of alchemy is this, and who but a select few have been initiated into the illu-pie-nati? When we look at the macro view of a finished pie, we can see a complex system. But when we start breaking down how to actually build a pie, we start to see that maybe it's not as insurmountable as we first guessed. When we see that the best pie dough is four ingredients (flour, water, salt, and fat), we can get our heads around that. And finally believing all those pie dough recipes that told us to put the flour and salt and water and fat in the fridge and keeping the dough nice and chilled is a liberating moment. And if they weren't lying about the fridge thing, what else were they not lying about? Now, as we become a little more myopic, we can see that none of the steps are, in themselves, all that difficult. A good pie is just a long sequence of easy tasks done correctly. Read that last sentence again. When you articulate it, you can substitute the word *pie* for really anything.

What I love the most about Jessica's book is seeing her process of bringing these incredible works of imagination to life. Pie making is its own subset of craft, just like cake decorating, and getting to watch a master pie-smith put together such unusual and technically challenging pies definitely helps me to not only understand the process better, but ultimately makes me a better pie maker myself. I'm no slouch, but I would rank pie dough as being as finicky as chocolate on the complex-things-of-the-pastry-shop scale. Getting to understand how Jessica can make the skyline of Paris or a unicorn out of pie dough might not teach me how to do the exact same thing, but understanding how she treats her dough as a medium definitely helps me make better pie dough for my Dutch apple pie.

Good pie notwithstanding, there is also the joy of watching someone who is incredibly good at what they do. I have never seen pies like Jessica's in person—maybe from history books, when pie as art was more of a thing a couple centuries ago. A craft this specific has to be created from trial and error and imagination, and when that happens, when we learn by doing, we acquire empirical knowledge, which is the best kind. When an artist like Jessica makes a book about her art and craft that contains techniques that she learned by tinkering, the result

is a work that is specific and unique. Seeing each pie come to life through techniques worked out by the artist is a joy, and understanding the medium from her point of view is illuminating and fascinating in that we're not just learning how to make insanely cool pies, but we're also learning a process that Jessica invented—we're learning how to learn.

Words, words, words. Let's be honest. I wanna see dope pies. Don't get me wrong—I read this book cover to cover like a novel, and as a fellow craftsperson who makes art from flour and sugar and butter, I absorbed everything I could, but viscerally. I was looking at amazing pies and saying "wow" a lot. It's neat watching artists create. Watching someone's hands do things that they have done thousands of times is endlessly mesmerizing, and seeing the steps that get them from A to B only makes the finished product that much more impressive. Jessica's pies are a treat in every sense of the word, and I think the only question you'll still have about pie after you read *Pies Are Awesome* is, "Plain, slice of cheese, or à la mode?"

Duff Goldman
Pastry Chef and Owner of Charm City Cakes
Food Network Host and Judge
Author of *Super Good Baking for Kids*, *Duff Bakes*, and *Ace of Cakes*
www.CharmCityCakes.com
www.Duff.com

Introduction

Hi there! How's your day going? Good, I hope, and if not, well, what better way to turn it around than to spend a few hours playing with pie! I'm Jessica, though folks online call me ThePieous, and I'll be your Pie Art tour guide for the next two hundred pages or so. I'm here to introduce you to a world that has brought me so much joy over the years, and my hope is that once I've shared it with you, you'll be inspired to share it with others and pass that joy on, because who couldn't use a little more joy in their life? Especially when it comes in such a delicious package. Onward!

The Power of Pie

Power in a pastry, you ask? Yes indeedy! Across the globe, cultures, demographics, and political affiliations, people have a relationship with pies. Whether we are talking about the sweet pies of North America, the savory pies of Europe, South America's empanadas, or Asian Spring Festival pastries, we all have our favorite. Almost every family has a special recipe or technique handed down the generations, along with special memories associated with its version of this timeless, classic comfort food. For so many people around the world, pie means "home." Pie is one of the very few things we can almost all agree is unambiguously good. You might not be able to talk about world events with your family in the presence of kitchen utensils right now, but dang it, you can still bake (and eat) pies together!

How about a Little Art with Your Pie?

If you're holding this book, it's probably not a long shot to suggest that you already agree that *Pies Are Awesome*, but what about Pie Art? And just what is this new Pie Art thing all about anyway?

For starters, it's not new! Pie Art is actually one of the oldest forms of food art (check out the little history lesson about "OG" Pie Artists on page 12), but for a variety of reasons, it fell out of fashion about two hundred years ago, and the pie slowly started to adopt its "humble" persona. Don't get me wrong. There is nothing subpar about a simple, rustic, delicious, unadorned pie. But when we can combine that flaky, yummy, nostalgic flavor with a bit of artistic flair, lovingly crafted into a form custom designed to delight and amaze its intended recipient . . . well, that's just magic! "Playing with our food" is a pastime that has never lost its charm, and with the rise of social media, we've never had more access to inspiring examples of epic wedding cakes, pancake portraits, clever fruit sculptures, charming cupcake characters, etcetera, etcetera. We create these works of edible art for birthdays, weddings, special events, and even just regular rainy blah days, all with the noble intention of putting a smile on someone's face (OK, and maybe also making your snooty college roommate totally jelly of your awesome wedding dessert buffet).

We know we love pies, and we know we love blending visual arts and food to make friends and family happy, so why has Pie Art been so rare up until recently? I believe it boils down to these three challenges with pie dough:

1. **The ticking clock.** The fat in pie dough melts and makes the dough tough if it is worked with too long, so we have limited working time to make fancy decorations.

2. **Distortion in the oven.** Pie dough shrinks and puffs up unpredictably in the oven, so any detailed decorations get obliterated.

3. **Discoloration.** Pie dough is subject to enzymatic browning, so colored dough loses all its vibrancy in the oven.

These three challenges have been accepted as immutable pie dough truths for so long that few bakers have wanted to risk spending time creating with it as an artistic medium for fear of being disappointed. But I knew, once I saw the glorious woodcut illustrations of the epic pies at the feasts of medieval kings and queens, that there had to be a way around all these issues. I made it my mission to uncover all the old tricks (and develop a few new ones of my own), and now I'm ready to share everything I've learned with you!

Jessica with her signature Piescraper

"OG" Pie Art from Conrad Hagger's *Neues Saltzburgisches Koch-Buch*, published in 1719 (*Artokoloro / Alamy Stock Photo*)

The "OG" Pie Artists

Far from "messing with an American classic," Pie Art is actually taking us back to an old, old, old skool pastry tradition: the novelty pie course.

To show off how awesome they were to their basic guests, kings, queens, and high-ranking nobility of the Middle Ages and Renaissance would order a special dinner course dedicated to the presentation of an epic, and I mean truly epic, Piescraper. Referred to as a subtlety, sotelty, sotelties, or entremet course, this pie was designed to both delight guests and show off how rich and influential the hosts were.

From the fourteenth to eighteenth centuries, the most famous of these epic pies contained living creatures, such as live birds, dancing girls, musicians, and tumblers. Some of the pies were fashioned into elaborate models of game animals and fantastical beasts, like dragons. Others depicted the host's castle and surrounding kingdom. Some of the pastries had inner pipework that made them gush fountains of wine or sauce, and some were even rigged with apparatuses to make the animals breathe fire! Talk about pie-oneering—these medieval bakers were the true OG Pie Artists!

I could write a whole book about these epic pies of history (and maybe I will one day), but for now, if you are interested in learning more, check out the resources listed on my website and social media to head on down that historical rabbit hole.

My Pie Art Journey

At this point, you may be wondering what qualifies me to be speaking to you about pie anyway? Well, believe it or not, just a few years ago I didn't even know how to crack an egg . . . it's true! The only time I ever turned my oven on prior to 2016 was to bake polymer-clay figures. For family potlucks, I was always told to "just bring the buns." I have an art-school degree, but "food art" was unfortunately not one of the available streams (though it totally should be). Fast-forward to 2016, when a New Year's resolution to not eat any sugar for one year drove me to learn to bake my own pies, and I slowly morphed from using my oven for only decorative art to using it for delicious art! Combining my love of science and craft, I trialed and errored my way through five years of baking experiments, determined to uncover the limits and full potential of this new crusty medium and share my discoveries with the world. Along the way, I've been fortunate to have my pies featured in hundreds of publications and my videos viewed by millions of people. Pies have taken me to the Food Network and the *TODAY* show as a pie judge and allowed me to meet and work with all sorts of inspiring and über-talented people! I've had so much fun. But if my time in this field has taught me anything, it's that there's always more to learn and discover.

You can learn more about me and my background on page 240, but let's get back to talking about you.

Your Pie Art Journey

Pie Art is not only the uncovering of a lost art form, but it's also a way of expressing our love of food and pop culture; discovering new cultures, new flavors, and new techniques; stretching ourselves creatively and intellectually; providing special dessert treats for the health-conscious; meeting weird and wonderful people; bonding with the next generation and passing on our love of baking; and, most of all, having fun! Playing around with Pie Art is going to be a lot of delicious fun for you, and it'll be even more fun if you can skip over all the un-fun learning-curve bits that I had to figure out the hard way—which is, of course, why I wrote this book!

It's Pie Time!

As much as I love creating in this medium, the best part of it all is sharing with other people and seeing their reactions when I present them with a custom-designed pie lovingly crafted with them in mind. And I want you to experience that too! So I've developed pie designs for many different special occasions on which you might gather with your loved ones, and together we walk through, step by step, how to create and customize them to your tastes. I want this book to give you the inspiration and confidence to really make these pies your own, using your favorite dough and filling recipes. And when you are ready to share your work, you'll find legions of supportive and appreciative fellow Pie Artists online waiting to welcome you and your crusty creations. And I can't wait to see what you make too!

At the end of the day, Pie Art is about joy. And joy always multiplies when we share it with other people. It is my sincere wish that this book will be just the beginning of your Pie Art journey, and that you, your friends and family, and everyone you love will experience firsthand just how awesome pies can be.

Happy Pie-oneering!
Jessica Leigh Clark-Bojin
(aka ThePieous)

PART 1

THE MAGIC OF PIE ART
(TECHNIQUES)

Pie dough is a unique and wonderful artistic medium, full of delicious potential. But just like working with clay, wood, marble, or any other artistic medium, it has its quirks. There are things it likes to do, and things it does *not* like to do.

The goal of this section of the book is to acquaint you with these quirks of pie dough, familiarize you with the different types of dough available to you, arm you with the knowledge needed to choose the right dough for your projects, and, finally, teach you all the skills you need to successfully coax your dough into doing your bidding without sacrificing texture or taste!

The Pie Art Learning Curve

As with any skill worth pursuing, there is a bit of a learning curve in mastering Pie Art techniques, but it's not as steep as you might imagine! Have a look at these two pies:

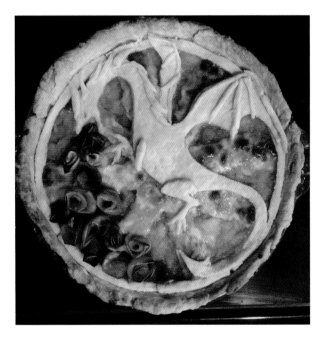

The image on the left was posted on my social media in April 2016, and it was the very first pie I ever made. A little funky by today's Pie Art standards (though it was considered "avant-garde" at the time). The image on the right is a pie I posted on my social media exactly one year later, in April 2017: a multitiered Piescraper. In one short year of practice, my pie game went from "Oh, cute" to "Daaayyymmn!!" . . . and so can yours! Have a read through the following sections, pick out a few projects to try, ask your questions in any of the Pie Art communities listed in the Resources section on page 228, and before you know it, your pies will be eliciting exclamations of "Daaayymmmn!" from your friends and family too.

Choosing the Right Pie Dough for You

There is no one magical dough for Pie Art—only the dough that is right for you.

Different projects will call for the prioritization of different dough properties. Sometimes your intended design will call the shots. Are you making a Pietrait (pie portrait) of someone? Then you'll need a dough that won't puff up much. Are you making a multitiered Piescraper? Then you'll need a sturdy dough that can support its own weight vertically. Other times, your recipe needs will call the shots. Has your Mum asked you to bake a pie using Grandma's special all-butter rough puff pastry? Then you'll need a design that works with puffy dough. Are you baking for a gluten-free friend? Then you'll need a design that can be cut out in place with no lifting. And still other times, completely unrelated factors will call the shots. Do you have to get to the party with a finished pie in an hour? Then you'll need to work with store-bought dough. Did your air conditioner break and it's 100°F (38°C) in your kitchen? Then you'll need to work with an all-shortening dough. Start by determining the "critical variable" for your project, and then work backward from there when choosing the right dough for you!

While I do recommend trying out all these different types of dough at some point in your pie-oneering career, we don't always have the time to experiment, and sometimes we just need something that we know will work. With that in mind, I have put together a little pie dough cheat sheet (ThePieous's Dough Comparison Chart on page 18) so that you can determine at a glance which dough type you are most likely to have success with for your specific Pie Art project.

Each of these pie doughs is composed of some form of fat, flour, and water, and, occasionally, a few bonus bits and bobs, like salt, sugar, egg, and binding agents. I'm not going to get heavy into the science of pie dough here, but if you are curious about that, check out the Resources section on page 228. Suffice it to say, the type of fat and flour, and the ratios, make a huuuuge difference to the properties of your dough. And this is by no means an exhaustive list! You can basically make something approximating pie dough out of any fat, flour, and liquid. Anything with a high fat content can fill that "fat" slot—avocado, cream cheese, olive oil, yogurt, almond paste. And vodka, bourbon, vinegar, vanilla extract, eggs, applesauce, beet juice, or just about anything wet can sub in for the water or liquid. There are many types of flours to experiment with too. Play around! Find out what's awesome and what's gross! Who knows, maybe you'll be the one to come up with the next top-secret family pie dough recipe!

Method Matters

There is one other thing I need to bring up before we dive into talking about each of these dough types specifically, and that is the *method* you use to create your dough. The way in which you combine ingredients—at what time, at what temperature, in what order, and so on—has just as big an impact on the final result as the ingredients themselves. When I say that a certain type of dough is pliable and easy to handle or has a flaky mouthfeel, that is only true when the dough is made perfectly according to its recipe. If you overmix an all-butter dough or allow puff-pastry butter to get melty before going in the oven, say good-bye to those "flaky mouthfeel" checkmarks in the

ThePieous's Dough Comparison Chart

	Widely Considered to Be Great-Tasting	Flaky Mouthfeel	Sturdy Dough for Vertical Panels	Doesn't Puff or Distort	Easy to Lift and Braid	Can Stand on Its Own Out of the Pan	Holds Sculpted Details Well	Long Working Time for Decorations	Easy to Make	Good for Special Diets	Good for Savory Pies (Not Sweet)
All-Butter Shortcrust	✓✓✓	✓✓✓			✓						✓✓
All-Shortening Shortcrust		✓	✓✓	✓✓	✓✓		✓✓	✓✓	✓	✓	✓
Half-Butter/Half-Shortening Shortcrust	✓	✓✓	✓	✓	✓		✓	✓	✓		✓
Half-Butter/Half-Lard Shortcrust	✓	✓✓	✓	✓	✓		✓	✓	✓		✓✓
All-Lard Shortcrust		✓	✓	✓	✓		✓	✓	✓		✓✓✓
Hot-Water Crust	✓		✓✓		✓✓✓	✓✓✓		✓✓✓	✓✓		✓✓✓
Puff Pastry	✓✓✓	✓✓✓			✓✓						✓✓
Rough Puff	✓✓	✓✓			✓						✓✓
Pasta Frolla/Pâte Sucrée	✓		✓✓✓	✓✓✓	✓	✓✓✓	✓✓✓	✓✓✓	✓✓✓		
Gluten-Free Dough										✓	✓
Pâte Brisée	✓✓	✓✓			✓	✓					✓✓
Pâte Sablée	✓			✓		✓			✓		

comparison chart! If your all-shortening dough is too dry or too cold when you roll it out, you'll lose those "easy to lift and braid" checkmarks.

But don't stress about it too much. A lot of this book is dedicated to how to still make awesome Pie Art even when your dough isn't perfect!

Dough Deets

All right! Let's take a quick look at the doughs in the comparison chart above.

All-Butter Shortcrust

This is the dough most people think about when they picture the classic American pie—light, flaky, buttery, and delicious. Butter has the lowest melting point

All-butter shortcrust

All-shortening shortcrust

Half-butter/half-shortening shortcrust

of all the "pie fats," so it is able to turn into steam quickly in the oven, creating those lovely air pockets in the dough. Unfortunately, it is because of this low melting point that butter is also the most notoriously difficult to work with when you want to create fancy decorations—you have to work extra fast to get your work done before it melts into the flour. And your designs are going to puff up and distort once the butter pockets turn to steam. No biggie for simple dough designs like lattices, flowers, and leaves, but a little more annoying in a portrait of your fave celebrity!

Pâte Brisée

This French pie dough is similar to the American all-butter shortcrust, but it's a little sturdier because the fat is incorporated a little more, and sometimes an egg is added (you will also see it referred to as pâte à foncer when an egg is added). The extra egg and butter incorporation mean slightly smaller air pockets and flakes, but it has the added benefit of being able to stand on its own outside of a tart or pie pan.

All-Shortening Shortcrust

Shortening has the lowest melting point of the fats—it still steams and creates air pockets like butter does, just way fewer of them. Because of the low melting point, all-shortening dough is great for creating fiddly Pie Art details, and those details remain after baking because it doesn't puff up as much. The trade-off is that shortening doesn't really taste like anything, though you can spiff it up a bit by adding an egg wash or a dash of bourbon or vanilla extract to the recipe. And bonus—it's vegan!

Half-Butter/Half-Shortening Shortcrust

For many, this is the "optimal" dough for Pie Art because you get the extra working time of shortening and still retain the butter taste. Each recipe is a little different—some call for a straight-up 50:50 ratio of the two fats, others 75:25—so it comes down to personal choice. Experiment and see what you think! I have included my favorite recipe on page 212.

All-Lard Shortcrust

Lard is another popular fat for making pie dough. Its working time is in between that of shortening and butter. Some people find it a little, well, "lardy" tasting. It can be great for savory pies, though! If you don't want your pie dough to smell like bacon, but you still want to use lard, make sure you ask your butcher for "leaf lard." That's a lard that comes from around the kidneys of the pig, and for some reason, it smells like nothing.

Half-Butter/Half-Lard Shortcrust

Like with the half-butter/half-shortening option, mixing and matching these fats can give you the desirable properties of both. Check out pie-baking superstar Kate McDermott's recipe on page 222! It is her go-to pie dough, and I can tell you firsthand that it is delicious.

Hot-Water Crust

Much more common in the UK than in the US, hot-water pie pastry is sturdy pie dough in which the fat is fully incorporated into the other ingredients because it is melted (on purpose!) with hot water. As you can imagine, this is a heck of a lot easier to create than

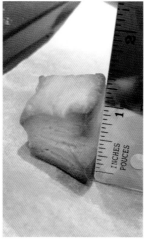

Rough puff

Pasta frolla

shortcrust—no fussing about with leaving unmelted tiny balls of the exact right size of fat intact. Because of the full incorporation of the fat, which is usually lard or butter, the crust is not as flaky, but it is able to be molded into tall shapes and can easily stand on its own outside of the pan.

Puff Pastry

Puff pastry is like all-butter shortcrust turned up to eleven. It is created through a process called laminating (Google it. It's a whole thing.). The gist is that it goes into the oven with lots of extra unmelted pockets of butter and creates multiple layers of air-pocket flakes. As you can imagine, this dough is disastrous at retaining fine Pie Art details, but it has amazing mouthfeel and tastes incredible.

Rough Puff

This dough is halfway between full puff pastry and all-butter shortcrust. Rather than being fully laminated with sheets of butter and folded over six or more times, rough puff only has to be folded over as is a couple of times. You still have to work extra quickly while it's cold to keep the butter from melting, but it's not as onerous a process as creating proper puff pastry.

Pasta Frolla/Pâte Sucrée

This sweet dough is sturdy and easy to work with, holds its shape amazingly well in the oven, and has a snappy, cookie-like mouthfeel. There are many variations of this type of dough, with varying levels of sweetness, but in all instances, the fat is incorporated more fully into the flour and there are usually eggs involved. It is a great dough for creating Pietrait likenesses, as it does not distort at all in the oven. It's also great for Piescrapers, as it can stand on its own outside of the pan with ease. The only downsides are the sweetness and the color. Compared to a typical butter shortcrust, it is a little anemic-looking, and, of course, it does not pair well with savory fillings. I have included a lightly sweet cookie dough recipe on page 216, and my friend and fellow Pie Artist Liz Joy shares an awesome keto variant on page 220!

Gluten-Free Dough

There are many different ways to make gluten-free dough, and it can be tricky to get the same flaky layers that we've come to expect from shortcrust pastry. But a few intrepid bakers have developed some amazing recipes that capture both the texture and the flavor we demand in our pies—such as the incredibly talented Courtney Ford, who graciously developed the gluten-free recipe on page 218 for this book! My family isn't gluten intolerant, but we've made her dough recipe for our pies loads of times because it is just that delicious. Because of the lack of gluten, this type of dough is a little more fragile and does not like being lifted up as much, so I will often opt for decorations that I can cut out on a baking sheet and bake in place rather than fancy latticework.

Gluten-free dough

Store-bought dough

Pâte Sablée

Another sweet French dough, pâte sablée has even more sugar than pâte sucrée, but it is named for its sandy texture rather than its sweetness. This dough has lots of butter and sugar and very little gluten. It is too crumbly for braiding and often needs to be pressed into a tart pan, but once it is baked, it is sturdy enough to stand on its own and has a yummy, rich, melt-in-your-mouth texture.

Store-Bought Dough

Finally, a quick word about store-bought, or "prefab," dough. Some people have strong feelings about store-bought doughs. I do not. My philosophy is "all pie is good pie" if it makes you and the recipient happy. Prefab pie doughs have different ingredient lists and properties. In general, most are designed to be pliable, easy to lift, braid, and so on, but still have a flaky mouthfeel by combining small amounts of binding agents, like xanthan gum, to replace some of the need for extra gluten. Because of the shelf life required of prefab dough, these doughs will all have some form of mold and bacteria inhibitors, and most will have a small amount of food coloring to mimic the color of a freshly made all-butter crust—particularly the prefab doughs made with lard, since this fat naturally has no color. Because of these elements (and the fact that you didn't make it yourself), pie purists will reject pies made with prefab dough as "not real" pies. I reject that rejection! All-butter

scratch-made pies taste amazing and I love them. But what if you want to make something special for your friend's birthday and you're not yet 100 percent confident in your abilities with scratch-made dough? What if you want to bring a pie but don't have enough time to make dough from scratch before the dinner party? What if you want to practice some of the new Pie Art techniques you just learned in this book and you don't want to waste a batch of the "good stuff" on your experiments? Or, heck, what if that's how your mum always made pies and you just like the taste of Pillsbury crusts? There are any number of reasons why prefab pie dough might be the right dough for you and your project on any particular day. Don't let anyone dough-shame you. I encourage you to experiment with all the different types of doughs I've mentioned in this section, but at the end of the day, you do(ugh) you!

If you would like specific recipes for any of the preceding dough types, or would like to learn more in-depth information about the science behind any of these doughs, check out the Resources section on page 228 (or leave me a comment or question on my Instagram posts @thepieous).

But if you're ready to start working with your new dough, let's talk about how to first take it for a test drive.

The Dough Test

There is no "good Pie Art dough" or "bad Pie Art dough," only dough we don't yet understand.

Most disappointment in the world of Pie Art comes from unanticipated results. Before you invest hours in crafting the perfect design, learn how *your* particular dough is going to behave in *your* particular oven. Then you can either adjust your design and strategy to match how your dough behaves or select a different dough that will better suit your existing design plans.

There are ten specific variables that I test for in my "dough tests," and I perform them the same way every time so that I have clear benchmarks against which to judge future doughs.

Now let's test some of those doughs we talked about in the last section and see what happens!

Remember, just because your dough "fails" these tests doesn't mean it's bad dough; it just means you are going to have to work a little harder and pay more attention to the techniques you use when working with it.

Bake Times

A word about bake times for your tests. In general, doughs that are more prone to puffing up do better with a higher temperature at first to shock them into shape—for Pie Art applications, we want the outside of a naturally puffy dough to cook and solidify before the inside to stop the spread, and high temperatures

All-butter dough test

Pasta frolla dough test

help us accomplish that. Dough that naturally keeps its shape (like pasta frolla) can start at a lower temperature and safely bake more evenly throughout. Experiment with different temperatures and bake times on scraps of dough and see what happens! I generally like to bake shortcrust pastry at 400°/425°F (205°/220°C; gas mark 6/7), and less flaky/puffy doughs at 350°/375°F (175°/190°C; gas mark 4/5).

ThePieous's Dough Test

Variable	What I'm Trying to Learn	Testing Methodology
Cutting Ease	If I drag my blade through the dough, will it cut cleanly, or am I going to have to use the special Press, Don't Pull method for cutting difficult dough on page 42? How easy is it to cut after 10 minutes, 15 minutes, half an hour? How often am I going to have to rechill it?	Roll out a small test piece of your dough on parchment, and let it sit out for 10 minutes. Then try to drag your knife through it and see if you get a clean line. If not, refer to Cutting Pie Dough on page 41 for tips on how to cut difficult dough.
Maneuverability	Can I lift this dough? Does it tear, stick, or crumble? Can I easily move pieces around, or will I have to cut everything in place and leave it there?	Try to lift pieces, and see if they stick or crack. If yes, refer to the tips in Rolling Out and Handling Pie Dough on page 37.
Braiding	Can I make a three-strand braid easily with this dough? How about a two-strand twist? How thin can I make the strips before they crack?	With your metal ruler, cut some strips of dough the smallest width you are able to lift without cracking. Attempt to make a three-strand braid, or if that is not possible, a two-strand twist.
Shrinkage & Distortion	How much will this dough shrink? Does it do so evenly? If I cut out geometric shapes, will they retain their sharp edges? If I make someone's face, will it puff up weirdly?	Cut out a 2-inch (5 cm) square with a ruler in place. Do not lift it—leave it where you cut it. Measure the height and depth with your ruler and photograph it for future reference.
Scored-Detail Retention	When I score a line in the dough, does it puff up and heal/disappear, or can I still see it clearly after baking? Do lines scored halfway through the dough split and separate after baking?	Cut out a rectangle of dough. Score your name on the dough with a toothpick or fondant sculpting tool. Score a line halfway through the dough with your ruler.
Molded-Detail Retention	If I make molded pieces of dough using a fondant mold, will the detail puff up and disappear after baking? How easy is it to get the raw dough pieces out of the floured mold?	Create a few molded pieces from a silicone mold.
Sculpted-Layers Retention	Can I easily blend multiple layers of dough together? Do they join together as one when pasted with pasteurized egg whites (see page 28), or do they stay separated?	With pasteurized whites (see page 28), paste together three layers of dough, and then score a line through them. See if they come apart in the oven.
Dough Color	Does it have a nice appetizing color naturally postbake or is it kind of anemic-looking? Does whole egg wash make a difference?	Cut out another small rectangle. Paint half of it with whole egg wash (or the wash of your choice).
Pigment Bleed	Do I need to do a lot of extra work prepping the surface to prevent feathering and beading of pigment painted on this dough, or is it easy to paint?	Paint some text on the square dough piece with vanilla wash (see Jessica's Tip on page 45)..
Bake Time	How long does this dough take to bake at ⅛-inch (3 mm) and ¼-inch (6 mm) thickness? How much do I need to adjust the bake time for different thicknesses of this dough? Do thin parts get burned to a crisp while the three-layer-thick piece is still raw? Does it spread out more when I bake it at a lower temperature? Does freezing it first, then baking at a higher temperature, stop the spread?	Bake your test pieces for 6 minutes to start, and then watch and record what they look like each minute after that, up to a maximum of 14 minutes. For flaky doughs, start at 400°F (200°C; gas mark 6); for crumbly doughs try, 350°F (175°C; gas mark 4). Every oven is different, so experiment!

Lay out all these pieces on a parchment-lined baking sheet. Take a photograph before and after baking. Refer to your photos when creating the design for your Pie Art.

All-shortening dough test

Store-bought dough test

It's not about having the "perfect dough." It's about understanding what the dough you've got is going to do.

Extra Testing

If I have a specific project in mind with unique design challenges, I may throw in a few additional tests.

For example, if I want to use a certain dough to make a Piescraper, I may also perform an "overnight structural integrity test," for which I bake long strips of dough, attach them to a triangular dough prop with icing or sugar glue, and leave them out to see if they are still standing in the morning. You may want to test out other elements specific to your design too, such as the effect baking will have on a natural powder pigment or whether a new type of food paint will bleed or bead up on your dough. Any element you're unsure about is worth testing before you invest hours crafting the perfect work of Pie Art!

Overnight structural integrity test

Selecting Fillings, Moisture Barriers, Washes, Garnishes, and Edible Adhesives

We've talked about how to choose the pie dough that's right for you and your Pie Art project, but what about the stuff that goes inside of that dough? There are some other critical components that round off a work of Pie Art, and they can have just as much of an impact on the success of your project as the dough! Let's take a closer look at each of these components and the properties that will affect your pie.

Fillings

As many types of dough as there are for Pie Art, there are even more choices of fillings. Taste is one obvious factor that will influence your choice of filling, but beyond the taste, there are other factors that will determine the success of your pie. Some types of filling make a lot of steam and cause the tops of pies to dome up. Some have a lot of acid or a lot of moisture. Some need thickeners and others don't. Some can sit out on the counter for days, and others have to stay in the fridge. Some are lumpy, and others can be smoothed flat. Some need to be served cold, and others taste best warmed up.

Just like with your dough choice, the filling you choose comes down to:

- The impact on the visual design of your pie

- The taste and mouthfeel (very personal!)

- Dietry restrictions

Examples of fillings

Examples of fillings

• A host of other logistical factors, such as the difficulty or cost of procuring specific ingredients, the difficulty and time involved in making a particular filling, the ease of storing and transporting your pie, food safety regulations for certain ingredients at certain venues, and so on.

In choosing your filling, start with your "critical variable" and work backward from there. Which of the above variables is most important to you? Is it a special birthday pie for your best friend? Then maybe you should choose their favorite filling. Is it for an outdoor charity bake sale? Then choose the filling that will be able to safely sit out in the sun for the longest time. Do you need to make the pie a day or two in advance because of time constraints? Then choose a filling that is easy to freeze and reheat. Do you need a perfectly flat white surface to create the design you have in mind? Then go with a "pour-and-set" filling, like an icebox pie. Did you just get gifted twenty bushels of peaches from your aunt's orchard? Then guess who's making peach pie! Time, taste, transportation, appearance . . . When you start with the variable that is most important to you and work backward, you'll have the best chance of a successful Pie Art project. For more information on fillings and some recipes to get you started, see page 210. I include links to some of my favorite filling recipes in the Resources section on page 228.

Moisture Barriers

Some filling and dough combos need a bit of extra help to keep their shape and protect them from "soggy bottoms," and that's where our moisture barriers come in. A moisture barrier is any edible substance that you add on top of the bottom crust before you add the filling, with the intention of limiting moisture transfer from the filling to the crust. They can be simple, like painting a bit of whole egg wash onto the bottom crust a few minutes before adding the filling. Or they can be complex, like creating stratified layers of chocolate, praline, and almond paste to give your pie shell extra flavor, texture, and structural integrity. As with everything we talk about in this section, choosing the right moisture barrier comes down to what is going to mesh best with the rest of your project. Most people pick the crust and filling first, and then find the moisture barrier that will best complement those two, but nothing says you can't start with the moisture barrier and work your way out! Maybe you've been dying to try out some nifty entremet layers you saw on a baking show, so in that case, by all means design the rest of the pie around your fancy internal layers.

Washes

Washes, or glazes, are what you brush on top of your piecrust to act as a protective layer, enhance color, add shine, and help define details. When your recipe calls for a wash of of something, it is simply directing you to cover the entire surface of your dough evenly with a thin layer of a particular substance—usually applied with a pastry brush. Pasteurized egg whites (see page 28) and vanilla wash (see Jessica's Tip on page 45) are my go-to washes, and they come up a lot in this book, but there are so many more options that you can experiment with—sugar water, milk, whole egg, honey, almond milk. If you're curious about their impact on your particular dough, add them to your dough test and try them out before you commit to using them on your final design.

Garnishes

Garnishes is a catchall term for any elements not made from dough that will be added to your pie postbake. These could be carved fruit, sprinkles, sanding sugar, chocolate elements, molded sugar work, caramel flowers, marshmallows, crushed cookies, wafer-paper feathers or wings, and even fondant! There are so many cool options. Just make sure that whatever you choose will complement the taste of the pie as well as the look. Here are a few fun garnish options, along with some tips on their usage:

- A rainbow gradient of sanding sugar hit with a kitchen torch looks gorgeous on top of any pie. Just factor in the extra punch of sweetness all that sugar will add, and choose a less sweet filling to pair it with so that you don't give your pie recipients an overload of carbs!

- Milk chocolate–piped butterflies are a lovely addition to a chocolate silk pie with meringue topping, but they might be a little gross on a pumpkin or lemon pie!

- Fresh herb leaves make a beautiful ornament around a pastry tree on top of a mac 'n' cheese pie, but be sure to choose leaves that complement the cheesy flavor. Parsley and basil, yes. Mint, no!

- Crushed pretzels look great as an edge trim on a peanut butter or chocolate pie and add a nice crunch, if you add them just before serving. If you add them the day before (or, God forbid, stick them in the fridge), they will have time to absorb moisture and go "bendy." Biting into a mouthful of bendy pretzels might not be the grossest thing in the world, but it's up there.

Examples of garnishes

Example of garnish

adhesives to defy gravity and adhere decorations to the sides of pies; support props to vertical dough panels; 3-D dough panels together; fruit, sprinkles, and other edible decorations to pies postbake; and any edible thing to any other edible thing when they don't naturally want to stick together!

Throughout the projects in this book, pasteurized egg whites (or almond milk if making a vegan pie) is recommended to attach unbaked dough layers to one another, but there are many other options when it comes to edible adhesives. Here is my (inexhaustive) list of some edible adhesives I have used, from weakest hold to strongest:

- Whole egg or egg white wash (prebake only)

- Meringue

- Sugar glue (such as Wilton Dab-N-Hold Edible Adhesive)

- Melted chocolate

- Melted candy melts or chocolate melting wafers

- Royal icing

- Isomalt (keep in mind that no one actually wants to eat this!)

Sometimes "hold strength" will be the determining factor for your project, and other times the flavor and mouthfeel of the adhesive will be most important to you. Experiment with different types and find your favorites!

- Whipped cream is one of those delicious garnishes with a ticking clock, and it looks gorgeous only if added just before serving. You can extend its life a little with some sneaky food-safe freeze spray, though!

Edible Adhesives

Edible adhesives have many uses in Pie Art, and allow us to push the boundaries of what pastry is capable of doing on its own. We can use these

There are a lot of factors to consider in selecting your dough, your filling, your moisture barrier, your garnish, and your edible adhesive, but don't get too hung up on making perfect choices. I find that experimentation leads to awesome discoveries just as often as it leads to gross messes, so have fun and try something new! Who knows, maybe you'll discover the next great trend in the world of Pie Art.

Why Pasteurized Egg Whites?

When egg whites are used as a blending medium, they come into greater contact with your hands and tools than they do when you are just cracking an egg into a mixing bowl. *Salmonella* bacteria present in eggs can make you and your family incredibly sick, so don't use raw unpasteurized eggs for this type of work! You can find pasteurized egg whites in cartons at the grocery store. I like to use Burnbrae Farms Naturegg Simply Egg Whites.

Pie Art Trends

Wait, did that last page say that there are "trends" in the world of Pie Art? You betcha! Just as there are different styles of cake art, there are different styles of Pie Art too, and more are being invented every day.

Whether you just want to quickly "spiff up" the pies you sell at the farmers market with an extra 15 minutes of decorative work or you want to create the most epic wedding pie buffet the world has ever seen and get written up in all the magazines, there is a Pie Art style for you.

Traditional Styles

There are a number of basic decorative pie formats that you are probably already familiar with:

- Lattice pies with assorted woven patterns
- Double-crust pies with decorative vents
- Open-face pies and tarts with decorative trim and toppings
- Hand pies with decorative cutouts
- Pie pops (simple small pies on sticks)
- Pies with ceramic "pie bird" steam vents

Any of these pies can be enhanced by using the techniques in this book, and you can achieve beautiful results in just a few minutes by adding simple decorative touches like flower and leaf appliqués or by stenciling pretty patterns with cinnamon.

My Experiments

While the traditional pie styles can give you gorgeous results, sometimes you want to kick your Pie Art up a notch. This is particularly true for occasions when you want your pie to function as a buffet centerpiece, visible from across the room. Weddings, epic birthdays, big corporate events, and times when you really need to "wow" someone

Jessica's experiments

Jessica's experiments

may be best served with one of my more recent Pie Art inventions (and I'm sorry/not sorry about all the following pie puns):

- **Piescrapers:** Multitiered gravity-defying pies

- **Pietraits:** Portrait pies of your best buddies or fave celebs

- **PieKabobs:** The ultimate pie sampler party food

- **Pie dolls:** Cake dolls have nothing on pie dolls!

- **Piepets:** Pie puppets, for those times when you want to play with your food

- **Glow pies:** My edible UV-reactive secret recipe for conveying secret pastry messages at pie raves

Other Pie-oneers' Inventions

I'm not the only one out there pushing the boundaries of pastry potential. You can find inspiration online from some of my Pie Art colleagues who've been pie-oneering their own awesome trends:

- Liz Joy, aka @inspiredtotaste (inspiredtotaste.com), popularized the cookie crust pie and has blown us all away with her incredible detail and design flair.

- Lauren Ko, who goes by @lokokitchen (lokokitchen.com), invented the "spoke pie," a brilliant new take on the traditional lattice that has a wholly unique look and is doable by even baking noobs.

- Julie Jones can be found @julie_jonesuk (juliejones.online), along with her stunning floral and romantic pie and tart designs.

- Karin Pfeiff Boschek, aka @karinpfeiffboschek (ourdeliciousfood.com), has taken geometric pie design to levels unfathomable just a few years ago.

- Chef Calum Franklin of the Holborn Dining Room is making old-skool hot-water crust pies sexy again. Check it out @chefcalum (holborndiningroom.com /pie-room).

- Rita Strati, an architect and baker who runs @stratiatelier (stratiatelierdellapastafrolla.com), is a genius at using colored pastry combinations to create the most beautiful layered compositions.

- Elisabetta Corneo, who goes by @artefrolla (stratiatelierdellapastafrolla.com), is an absolute wizard with Italian pasta frolla dough. She teaches classes on her many jaw-dropping techniques for adding dimension to the standard tart shell.

There are a lot more Pie Artists I could highlight (and I do in The Pie Art Family section on page 230).

You should be starting to get a feel for the Pie Art styles available to you. And don't for a second think there isn't room for more discoveries! I've just started tinkering with interactive pies and kinetic-motion pies and working with custom-shaped pie pans myself. And who knows what's percolating in your noggin right now? The Pie Art Revival is only five years old at this point, so just imagine what creative pastry awesomeness will be out there in the next five, ten, or twenty years!

Supplies

All right, we're pumped. We're ready to get our hands dirty and start making some Pie Art pastry magic. But is there anything other than our hands that we're going to need?

The truth is, we really don't *need* a lot of stuff to make cool Pie Art. But you're probably going to *want* a bunch of this stuff. While most of these tools aren't mission critical, it is fun to play around with different tools, supplies, and other time-saving devices, especially if you are an art-supply and gadget nerd like me!

This section lists the "must-have," the "nice-to-have," and the bonus "expensive-and-hard-to-get-but-supercool-items-you'll-ask-for-if-you've-got-a-birthday-coming-up-or-something" tools. I also mention the basic baking supplies (you probably have all this stuff already) and some of my favorite edible decorative components.

Before we dive into the lists, a caveat: When I started out with Pie Art, my decorating arsenal was composed wholly of my hands and a toothpick. That's it. And honestly, with just those two things, I would be able to create half of the projects in this book (though it'd be a pain in the butt). So don't get too hung up on whether or not you have all the latest toys before you get started. You can easily add to your toolbox as you go, and your friends and family will have no trouble buying you presents for the foreseeable future!

Pie Art Must-Haves

These are the elements that I use every day:

- Food-safe precision blade
- Flexible cutting mats
- Baking sheets
- Parchment paper
- Fondant sculpting tool (or toothpick)
- Cake lifter
- Pastry brush
- Food-safe art brushes
- Brown gel food color
- Ramekins or other small containers
- Stainless-steel rulers (without a cork backing)

Must-have supplies

Nice-to-have supplies

Pie Art Nice-to-Haves

These are the super-handy tools to start collecting:

- Food-safe acetate stencils
- Gel and powder food colors
- Food-safe silicone fondant molds
- Sugar glue (such as Wilton Dab-N-Hold Edible Adhesive)
- Silicone impression molds
- Silicone cake molds
- Plunger cutters of different shapes
- Impression sticks/trim cutters
- Cookie cutters
- Mini rolling pin
- Pie pop sticks
- Piping bags
- Additional food-safe sculpting tools
- Single-use sponge brushes
- Crimped pastry wheel
- Paper, pencil, and scissors for paper templates
- Food-safe found objects for impressions

Next-level supplies

Pie Art Next Level

Do you have a big birthday coming up?

- Cricut stencil-cutting machine
- Food-safe cold spray (the electronics kind, not the automotive kind)
- Chocolate melter
- Silicone impression mats
- Tart rings of assorted shapes
- Perforated silicone baking mat (I like Silikomart's air mat)
- Silicone impression strips (tart ring inserts) (I like Silikomart brand)
- Fancy dessert stands
- Fancy pie servers
- Large-capacity food processor
- Stand mixer (such as KitchenAid brand)
- Oven thermometer

 Jessica's Tip

You'll notice I repeat the term *food-safe* a lot. That's because many crafting items are made of plastics that have not been tested on food items and may leach plastic particles into your food (gross!). So be sure to choose molds and stencils made from materials that are meant to come in contact with food. When in doubt, call the manufacturer and ask if an item is food-safe!

Basic Baking Stuff

You probably already have all of this, but just in case . . .

- Digital kitchen scale (If you buy nothing else, please buy one of these!)
- Metal pie pan
- Metal mixing bowls
- Rubber spatula
- Metal spatula
- Pastry blender/cutter
- Flour sieve
- Rolling pin with height guides
- Paper towels
- Measuring spoons
- Oven mitts

Basic baking stuff

Decorating Ingredients

These are fun edibles (no, not that kind):

- Cheap vanilla or almond extract
- Cheap vodka
- Pasteurized egg whites (see page 28)
- Shake can of flour
- Food paints
- Luster dusts
- Sanding sugars
- Different types of sprinkles
- Crushed nuts and other "crunch" garnishes
- Maraschino cherries
- CakePlay Isomalt Nibs
- Melting chocolate
- Candied rose petals

Decorating ingredients

- Meringue powder
- Agar-agar
- Chocolate chips
- Marshmallows

In the Resources section on page 220, I provide links to the places where you can purchase all these items, but your local hobby store or specialty-food/baking-supply store should also have most of what you need. And remember, all you really need to get started is your own two hands and something small and poke-y!

Setting Up Your Workspace

Now that you've got all of your supplies ready to go, it's time to start setting yourself up for success, and setting up your workspace!

Confession: I'm not the most organized human on the planet when it comes to most other aspects of my life. But when it comes to Pie Art projects, I'm always on the ball. Why? Because of that nagging little "working time" variable in ThePieous's Dough Comparison Chart on page 18. From the moment we roll out our dough, the clock starts ticking and we want to be able to work as efficiently as possible, putting all of our effort into getting our design done, and none of it into tracking down supplies, making stencils, or remembering steps!

There are two things I do before I start working on any Pie Art project: create a to-do checklist and set up my workspace mise en place.

The first one is simple. I create a (usually handwritten) list of all the steps I need to complete for the particular project, in the order I need to complete them. When I'm baking on a deadline and it's three o'clock in the morning, I can't always rely on my brain to be at its sharpest. Even obvious things can slip my mind when I'm a bit frazzled. So I write them all out. Then all I have to do is follow the directions one at a time, and the rest of my brain is free to zonk out and absorb trash TV while I work!

The second item, working mise en place, just means I put out everything I am going to need for the entire project in its proper place before I start working. But what is the "proper place," and what is "everything"? Let's take a look at my workspace setup.

Your Pie Art Workspace Zones

Your Pie Art workspace comprises several specific zones: the main dough stage, the dough-prep area, wet supplies, tools, and clean space for notebooks and electronics.

A Word about Parchment Paper

Before we dive into our workspace setup, it is important to talk about parchment paper. You'll notice that every technique tutorial and project in this book calls for you to roll out your dough directly onto a piece of parchment paper—ideally on top of a flexible cutting mat. Why? Because the dough we use for our Pie Art should be handled as little as humanly possible, and always keeping our dough on a piece of parchment paper allows us to lift our dough without risk of stretching or tearing it. When our dough is on a parchment-lined flexible cutting mat, we can easily pop it into the freezer to cool down, easily transfer it to a baking sheet, and easily move it out of the way when working on multiple pies without fear of damaging it. To save myself time, I always keep a box of precut sheets on hand!

The Main Dough Stage

The area in the center front is for dough that we do not lift and goes directly into the oven as is. Here we always work on a flexible cutting mat lined with parchment. When we need to chill our dough, we lift both the cutting mat and parchment and place them in the freezer. When the project is complete, the baking tray slips underneath both the cutting mat and parchment, and then the cutting mat is carefully pulled out, thus ensuring our dough never stretches or distorts on its way to the oven.

The Dough-Prep Area

Set up this area on the right if you are right-handed or on the left if you are left-handed. This is where we work with dough that will be transferred to the main stage. Cut out shapes, strips for lattices, molded pieces, and so on here. These can be prepped directly on a flexible cutting mat, without the parchment, but feel free to add some parchment on top anyway if you don't feel like washing your cutting mats.

Wet Supplies

To the left, we keep our wet supplies, also on top of a flexible cutting mat for easy cleanup. These include a ramekin of pasteurized egg whites (see page 28), a couple of ramekins for mixing your edible emulsifier and pigment (see Coloring Pie Dough on page 44), and your pigments and used brushes. I keep a couple of paper towels under the pigments to absorb any leaks, minimize cross contamination, and wipe my brushes.

Tools

I store my clean tools, such as rulers, knives, molds, cookie cutters, and toothpicks, above my main dough stage and only bring them down as needed. Once they're used, I put them in the sink for handwashing and to get them out of the way.

Clean Space

On either side above my cutting mats, I keep a clean space for my notebook, any devices I'm using for reference images, my "entertainment laptop" for streaming movies or music while I work, and any paper templates I will be using. Paper templates are especially sensitive to moisture, so keep them well away from the action until they are needed. Oh, and make sure you remember to prep and cut them all out before you get started!

The Room You're In

We've talked about how to set up the workspace that's in front of us on the table or counter, but don't forget about prepping your larger work environment too! Is it too hot in your kitchen? Open a window, set up a fan, or crank the AC before you begin. Are you going to get chilly at some point? Go get your sweater now. What about music or TV? Do you want to chillax with some classical while you work? Or maybe throw a trashy '80s rom-com on the laptop in the background to keep you awake through an all-night bake session? (Have I watched every '80s movie on Netflix while baking? Yes. Yes, I have.)

Bottom line: Once your dough is out, it's all about the dough. Don't waste precious minutes searching for items or setting things up. Spend as much time, if not more, planning out your project as you do making it, and your future self will thank you!

Rolling Out and Handling Pie Dough

Let's talk about a few of my tips and tricks for treating pie dough right and ensuring it will treat us right in return.

First things first, feel free to make your pie dough any ol' way that makes you happy. The method that you use to make your pie dough isn't going to have a huge impact on your finished product one way or the other, but the method that you use to *roll out* and *handle* your dough will!

Rolling Out Pie Dough

The method you use to roll out your pie dough will have a big impact on how well your dough will hold its shape in the oven, and how much detail you can achieve in your Pie Art projects. I designed the steps below to minimize dough stretching and to relax gluten formation—both are enemies of predictable Pie Art results!

1. Start by portioning out your dough balls onto sheets of plastic wrap on your counter. You'll need one grapefruit-size lump for your base pie and two orange-size lumps for your top decorations.

2. Place another piece of plastic wrap on top of each of the balls, and using the heel of your palm, smoosh the balls into roughly 1-inch-thick (2.5 cm) disks.

3. Grab a rolling pin and roll the dough disks through the plastic wrap to about ¼-inch (6 mm) thickness, trying to keep the circle shape even by changing the direction of your rolling and patting in the edges by holding your hand perpendicular to the dough to keep it from cracking as you go. A rolling pin with height guides is handy but not necessary for this task.

4. Place the heels of your hands on the counter so that your hands are perpendicular to the disk of dough. Gently slide your hands inward and pat the edges of the disk to flatten out any cracks.

5. Wrap the plastic around the edges of your dough, making sure there is a seal all the way around. You may need to add another piece of plastic wrap if the dough is sticking out the edges of the plastic.

6. Stack up all your doughs and pop them in a freezer bag, or just add another layer of plastic wrap around them. Place them in the fridge on a flexible cutting mat and chill for at least 2 hours, or up to overnight, before you use the dough.

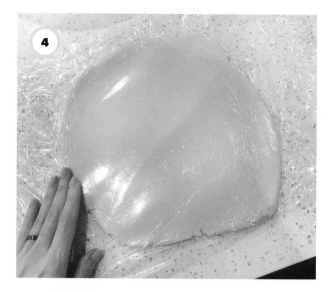

This process may look a little different from traditional pie dough instructions. Why do I roll out my dough almost all the way before I chill it, when practically everyone else tells you to just make "flattened disks" instead? There are a few reasons:

- Newly created dough is warm and pliable, and therefore much easier to roll out into the exact shape you want.

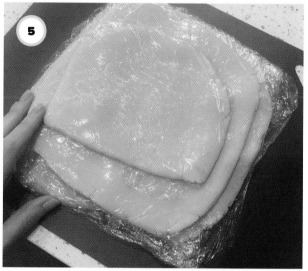

- Rolling out your dough *and then* chilling it gives the gluten a chance to relax and contract before you work with it, so your decorations don't get as distorted in the oven (see the photo of the two dough circles on page 40).

- Disks of chilled pie dough have to warm up before you can roll them out. While you wait for your dough to get to "roll-out temp," the fat is melting and your working time is ticking away. If your dough is pretty dang close to the thickness you want anyway, it'll be much colder when you start working with it.

- Rolling out the dough to ⅛-inch (3 mm) thickness before chilling it is a little too thin, and it can become brittle and crack when it is chilled overnight. A thickness of ¼ inch (6 mm) is kind of the sweet spot for me—not too fragile chilling in the fridge, not too onerous to roll out to the perfect thickness the next day.

When you are ready to work, simply take the flattened doughs out of the fridge, let them warm up for a minute, and then roll them out to their final thickness of ⅛ inch (3 mm) on a parchment-lined flexible cutting mat. You can either use a bit of flour here or roll through the plastic wrap, whichever you prefer.

This method of rolling out and prepping dough for Pie Art will give you the best chance for success when it comes to creating your top decorations. But if you're really keen on your existing method of rolling and chilling, you can always do the old ball/disk thing for your base pie dough, and just use my method for the dough you'll be using for the top decorations.

Handling Pie Dough

Now, once you've got your dough rolled out and you're ready to rock and roll, here are a few tips on handling that dough to take the stress out of the process and extend your work time.

You may have noticed the term "working time" in ThePieous's Dough Comparison Chart on page 18. This refers to how long you have before the fat in your dough starts to melt and your dough becomes soft, is hard to cut, and starts to lose its ability to form "flakes," or air pockets, in the oven. All pie dough is susceptible to heat and humidity, and you want to make sure that your kitchen and workspace, hands, tools, and so on are all as chilly-willy as possible, and when you are working with butter-based doughs, this is doubly important. Butter melts at a temperature of around 100°F (38°C), which is basically the same temperature as your hands. Yikes! Shortening like Crisco has a melting point of 111°F (44°C). If your hands are that temperature, stop making pies and go to the emergency room. But if you are not currently suffering from malaria, you'll be able to work with shortening-based dough for quite a long time before you need to rechill it. Lard-based doughs, combo doughs like half-butter/half-shortening, and specialty-fat doughs like nut butter or avocado fat doughs are all somewhere in the middle.

Give your dough a time-out to chillax in the freezer every 15 to 30 minutes.

All of the doughs will eventually absorb heat from their environment and start to become tricky to work with. For butter dough, this may happen in as little as 10 minutes; for shortening, maybe 30 minutes or more. Regardless of which dough you are working with, at some point you are probably going to want to add a few more minutes (or maybe hours!) to the clock. How do you do it? You already know from the discussion on Setting Up Your Workspace on page 35 that you should roll out your dough for Pie Art onto sheets of parchment paper (ideally on flexible cutting mats), and not directly on the countertop. This is so that as you're working and noticing that your dough is getting a little sweaty and harder to cut, you can pick up the whole shebang and pop it into the freezer for 2 minutes to let it settle down. You can repeat this process as many times as you like until you are finished with your design and ready to bake!

Controlling the temperature of the dough's environment and working on a parchment-lined flexible cutting mat so that you can rechill your dough as needed are two critical methods for keeping your dough tamed. The following techniques have to do with how to handle the dough directly once everything is set up.

I always tell students and followers of mine who are struggling with temperamental dough this: once you've rolled out pie dough, don't touch it, don't lift it, and NEVER stretch it.

But let's be honest, you're totally going to do all those things.

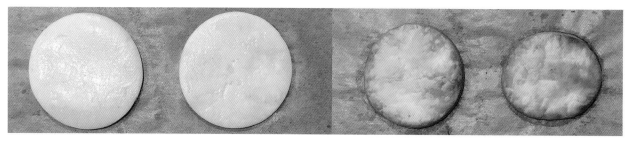

The baking outcomes of dough that was cut in place (left) versus dough that was lifted (right)

Why are touching, lifting, and stretching your dough so bad? Three main reasons:

1. Touching your dough with your hands warms it up.

2. If your dough is fussy, lifting it may cause it to tear, deform, crack, or otherwise go awry.

3. Stretching pieces of your dough also causes the gluten strands inside to stretch (these are microscopic elastic bands inside your dough that hold it all together). Once you stop stretching the dough, the gluten strands slowly contract to how they were, but it takes some time. Imagine what will happen to your carefully cutout shapes if you first stretched out the dough, then made your cuts, then baked them. Actually, you don't have to imagine. Just look at the photo at the top of the page. The circle on the right was cut after the dough had been lifted up and left to hang for a second. The circle on the left was cut from a piece of dough that was never lifted up from the parchment it was rolled out on. As you can see, the circle of dough that was lifted and stretched has deformed into an oval shape in the oven, and is no longer perfectly round because of the gluten-strand contraction. It's not such a big deal if it's just a flower or leaf cutout, but think how funky things could get if this were a portrait of someone! Cutting elements in place and leaving them right where they are on the parchment sheet until they've baked are the best ways to ensure no part of your design becomes misshapen in the oven.

All right, you know you should limit your handling of the dough. But what if you *have* to lift something? Say, to place cutout letters on top of another part of the pie or to place an entire top decoration onto a base pie? I've gotcha covered. If you know you are going to need to lift a component later, roll out that dough directly on a flexible cutting mat (you don't have to worry about parchment paper here), cut out your pieces, and then freeze them solid. Now you can easily lift them up and move them over with a spatula or cake lifter. Freezing your work will not hurt *unpainted* pie dough at all (painted pie dough can feather and spread out a little if it is in there too long).

Here are some final tips:

• If you accidentally stretch something out, try to unstretch it by gently tapping it back into the shape it was. This works okay for flowers, border trim, and simple shapes, but not so much for faces.

• On hot days, don't preheat your oven until your top decoration is done and chilling in the fridge. The last thing you need while making Pie Art is extra heat in the kitchen!

• If you need to take a break from your work to tend to something else, you can coat your design in pasteurized egg whites (see page 28), lightly pat plastic wrap over the whole surface (not forgetting the edges), and stick it in the freezer on your parchment-lined flexible cutting mat for up to 24 hours. Then you can pick up where you left off when you are ready to get back to it.

• To get your base pie dough into your pie pan, don't try to lift it at all. Simply place the pan on the dough upside down, and then flip the cutting mat, parchment, dough, and pie pan right side up again. All you have to do is carefully peel away the parchment and let the dough sink into the pan on its own. There is no stretching or tearing, even for fragile dough like gluten-free!

Now that we know how to treat our dough right, we're ready to dive into the artsy fun part and start learning some do(ugh)pe skillz!

Cutting Pie Dough

One of the questions I get asked most frequently about my Pie Art is, "How do you manage to cut such fine details out of pie dough?" Followed by some combination of "My edges are always so scruffy and cracked when I try to cut dough!" or "My shapes always get smooshed when I try to cut tiny things!" or "My dough is too sticky/dry/warm/crumbly to cut!" And generally capped off with "My dough must just suck!"

But as we've already discussed, there really is no such thing as a "sucky" dough, just sucky ways of handling dough or, at least, ways of handling dough that won't get us the results we're looking for!

So if it's not about the dough itself, is there a trick to cutting dough for Pie Art that will allow us to achieve that fine detail folks ask about? Heck yes, there is! Four tricks, in fact.

Jessica's Four Tricks for Cutting Pie Dough

I have developed four tricks to ensure that anyone can get supersharp detail out of even the stickiest, crumbliest, sweatiest dough, and they are as follows.

#1: Keep It Sharp

We've all got a drawerful of "sharp knives," but when it comes to pie dough, kitchen knives sadly won't cut it (ha!) for two reasons: the first reason is that they probably aren't sharp enough if you've been using them on other food, and the second reason is that their handles are not designed for tiny finesse work. Instead, what we need is a food-safe precision blade. What the heck is that? Basically, an X-ACTO knife that we can chuck in the dishwasher. They are supersharp and have nice grippy bodies that

make them as easy to use as a pen, and the sharp part of the blade is confined to the bottom inch (2.5 cm), so there's little danger of hurting yourself accidentally. The best place to buy these is in the cake-decorating section of hobby stores—any knife labeled "fondant cutting blade" will be food-safe and appropriate for pie dough. I personally like TIDI's PenBlade brand of blades because they retract when not in use (handy around kids) and can be thrown in the dishwasher (did I mention I'm lazy about dishes?). But choose whatever brand you have easy access to.

Why do you need such a sharp knife anyway? Two words: dough displacement. When you drag a knife through dough, the dough in front of the knife doesn't just disappear—it gets displaced (or smooshed) off to the sides of the cut. The duller your blade, the more surface area there is coming in contact with the dough, and the more dough there is to displace, which makes your cut scruffier.

#2: Keep It Cold

If you've spent any time working with pie dough, you've probably already figured out this trick for yourself! As pie dough starts to warm up and become more pliable, it becomes softer. Soft dough likes to go with the flow, and as we try to pull our knife through it, we'll notice that the dough starts to come along for the ride. Look at the photo at the top of page 42. The dough on the left was cut right after it came out of the fridge after a couple hours of chilling. The dough on the right was cut after it sat out on the counter in a warm kitchen for an hour. Big difference! To prevent drag in your pie dough

Cutting cold dough (left) versus warm dough (right)

as you cut, pop your work in the freezer for 2 minutes whenever you start to notice it is becoming more difficult to cut. If you're working with an all-butter dough or on a very warm day, you may have to do this a few times before you are finished with your Pie Art design, but fortunately, since you are working on a parchment-lined flexible cutting mat, and not directly on your counter, that's easy to do, right?

#3: Plan the Direction of Your Cuts

It's all well and good to say "just keep your dough super cold all the time," but let's be realistic; sometimes that's just not possible due to time constraints or our own impatience. But there is another technique we can employ to mitigate the effects of warm dough drag, and that is to plan the direction of our cuts. Since we know that the dough is going to follow along with the knife, we can strategically choose which direction that pull is going to go to minimize the impact on the shape we are trying to create.

Check out the star shape in the photos below. When you start in the center and move your knife outward, the drag makes the points of the star sharper. But if you go the other way, and cut toward

The correct direction to cut dough

the center, the drag causes the points of the star to get pulled inward and become rounded and lame. Keep this in mind when cutting out fiddly things like letters and shapes that you want to retain sharp corners.

Another tip for keeping our shapes sharp has to do with how we remove the bits of dough we don't need. We already know not to lift the shapes once we've cut them (unless they are frozen solid), but that also goes for the dough around the shape! Sometimes, no matter how careful we are, we might have a segment of dough that was not quite cut all the way through. Then if we try to peel away the excess dough, it pulls up a chunk of our carefully cutout shape, distorting it in the process. Instead, it is much safer to cut away this excess dough a chunk at a time, only removing it once it is safely detached from your shape.

The proper way to remove excess dough from around a cutout shape

#4: Press, Don't Pull

This last trick is the ultimate tool in dealing with "difficult" doughs. If our dough is very cold, we can get away with dragging our knife through the dough to cut it; however, if it is at all warm, sticky, crumbly, or in any way less than perfect, doing this will likely cause our dough to tear as we cut through it. Does this mean you can't cut sharp details out of your imperfect dough? No! It just means you have to cut it a different way by *pressing* rather than *pulling* your blade through it. This forces the dough displacement down instead of along the line of your cut.

You can either chop down with the edge of your precision blade, which is a great option for cutting straight segments, or you can poke your blade's point straight up and down like a sewing machine needle.

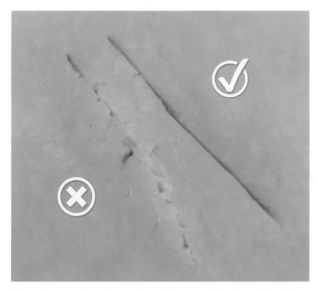

Jessica's Tip

If your blade is a little dull and you end up with "fluffy edges" anyway, just dab a bit of pasteurized egg whites (see page 28) onto your finger and gently smooth the edges back into place with the back of your fingernail.

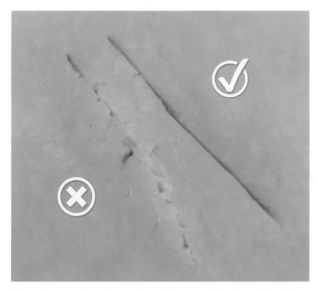

The outcomes of pressing versus pulling the blade through dough

I usually opt for the second technique (and say "poke poke poke poke" while I'm doing it), because it allows me to cut smooth curved lines. It takes a little longer to cut by pressing straight up and down rather than dragging, but you are guaranteed a clean cut no matter how warm your dough is!

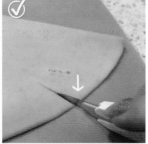

The press, don't pull technique

The Stainless-Steel Shortcut

The preceding four tricks are great for precision cutting of freehand shapes, but there is a faster way to cut pie dough when you only need to cut straight lines: the stainless-steel shortcut. This is just a fancy way of saying "use a ruler." I have a collection of food-safe stainless-steel rulers that I use for pretty much every Pie Art project. Make sure you buy one without a cork backing (because that's not food-safe) and with markings that go right to the edges. Run it through the dishwasher before your first use to remove any factory oils. I use my rulers to measure with, to cut straight lines for lattices, and to lift and move around frozen dough pieces. They are probably the most versatile tool in my decorating arsenal!

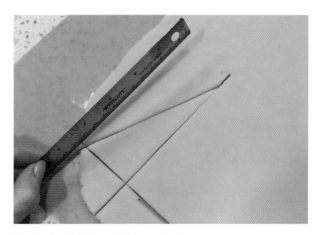

Cutting dough with a stainless-steel ruler

Now, if you combine these cutting tricks with the dough-handling tips from the previous section, you'll be well on your way to getting (and retaining) crazy-fine detail from your pie dough!

Coloring Pie Dough

Pie dough is beautiful on its own, and monochrome compositions can look great, but sometimes it's fun to add a little color. Heck, sometimes it's fun to add a lot of color!

Why don't we see this done more often with pies? I have a couple of theories, but the main reason, I believe, is that people have tried it in the past and were disappointed with the results. Pie dough is made with fat and water in an uneven mixture, which can cause colors to bead up or get streaky. Errant poofs of flour can get on your dough and stop the color from sticking. Natural pigments added to the dough can turn brown and lose their vibrancy in the oven. There are several challenges that would-be Technicolor Pie Artists may have faced on their own, but, fortunately, I have figured out, through trial and error (and error and error), some easy fixes for all of these glitches that will unlock a world of colorful pie-sibilities for you!

Is It Weird to Eat Colored Pie Dough?

Another reason some folks have been hesitant to add color to dough is that pie's rustic reputation is at odds with the bright colors of fondant and icing we see on cakes, cupcakes, and cookies. If you or the recipient of your pie falls into this camp, you can still use color; just stick to colors you find naturally in food (no blue or black)—choose browns, reds, oranges, yellows. Or add color a different way with colorful fruits, chocolates, or other edible bling, and leave the dough to shine on its own!

Edible Emulsifiers

I mentioned that pie dough is made of fat and water. Fat is essentially oil, and oil and water are not typically friends. So, when we use traditional food colors that are meant for more homogeneous surfaces, like fondant or icing, we can sometimes get wacky results! The pigment does not behave the same way when it's sitting on top of oil as it does when it's sitting on top of water. So what do we do? We introduce our secret weapon—a substance that forces the oil and water to play nicely with each other—our edible emulsifier.

What the heckaroony is an emulsifier, you ask? For our purposes, an edible emulsifier is any edible liquid substance that binds to both water and oil. The emulsifier coats the fat and water on the surface of the dough evenly and provides something else for the pigment to bond with. There are many edible liquids that can act as an emulsifying agent, but my top three faves are:

1. **Vanilla extract:** It has a nice flavor and gives the colors a bit of a rustic look.

2. **Almond extract:** It keeps the colors vibrant and offers a different taste.

3. **Vodka:** Used for savory pies, it keeps colors vibrant without any added flavor because it all burns off in the oven.

You can use any food-grade extract (don't use essential oils!) or liquid with some protein. Try using milk, almond milk, soy milk, orange extract, or edible lavender extract. All will have a slightly different look and consistency. You can even use a well-blended raw egg; it will give the color a shiny finish, although it is streakier to paint with because of the viscosity (aka lumpy snottiness).

The photo at the top of the opposite page shows what different emulsifying agents look like when used with some orange gel food color. From left to right are plain water, vanilla extract, vodka, and pasteurized egg whites (see page 28). Notice that the vanilla and vodka give the most even coverage, and the color mixed with plain water has beaded up in places.

Outcomes of different edible emulsifiers (from left to right): water, vanilla extract, vodka, pasteurized egg whites

Jessica's Tip

Vanilla wash is my top-secret pie-coloring trick. Okay, it's not top secret, but it is my go-to trick for retaining tiny sculpted details! Because pie dough puffs up in the oven, painstakingly sculpted, tiny details are often completely obliterated after baking. But, if you first give your pie a generous coating of vanilla extract (1 tablespoon) mixed with a tiny bit (a toothpick scoop) of brown gel food color—aka vanilla wash—the color will seep into the cracks of your design and lock in place when the heat of the oven hits it. The dough will still puff up, but the lines will remain visible, and your detail will be optically preserved! A vanilla wash is a great way to amp up the drama of a "rustic" pie design too, because postbake it does not read as a separately applied color but just looks like natural shadows.

Food-Safe Pigments

Now that you know how to get your pigment to stick to the dough, what sorts of pigments should you choose? Gel food colors, liquid colors, opaque icing colors, luster dusts, natural and artificial powder pigments, food color pens—so many options! They all behave a little differently, and each one works best when applied to the dough at different points—on either prebaked dough, premixed dough, or postbaked dough.

Prebaked Dough Color

The best time to add color is before the dough is baked. When you are properly using an emulsifier, the pigment gets the most even coverage at this stage, and any yucky taste from the pigment gets baked away in the oven. The baking process also makes the pigment colorfast, meaning it won't make your guests' teeth and tongues turn funky colors, and it won't run if the air is a bit humid.

Gel food colors work the best at this stage. Because they are more transparent, they absorb into the dough more and won't crack after baking. However, they are slightly transparent and can only be as light as the dough itself. If you want "lighter-than-dough" colors, you will have to mix them with a little bit (a toothpick scoop) of opaque white icing color.

To paint your dough with gel food colors, add 1½ teaspoons of vanilla extract (or the edible emulsifier of your choice) to a ceramic ramekin or tiny glass bowl, then dab a generous toothpick full of gel food color on the edge of the ramekin. Dip your brush into the vanilla at the bottom and then into the pigment on the side and paint away!

Premixed Dough Color

The next-best time to add color is before the dough has been mixed. You still get the benefit of (most of) the taste being baked away, and you can get quite bright colors with the artificial powder pigments. Just remember that pie dough does not like to be manhandled once the fat, water, and flour are combined, so do your color mixing *before* that point. Add liquid color to your water; add powder color to your flour. Make sure they are well combined individually, and *then* combine the wet and dry ingredients. Do NOT treat your dough like fondant and try to knead in the color. Well, I mean, you *can*, but then you'll end up with a helluva tough crust. This is not such a big deal if you're using a cookie dough or crumbly tart crust recipe, but it can be a disaster if you want a flaky shortcrust dough at the end. You can experiment with these pigments:

- **Juices:** Dragon fruit and beet juices will get quite brown postbake, but try them out!

- **Natural powders:** Chlorophyll, matcha, butterfly pea flower, and turmeric powders will also brown in the oven, but not as much as the liquid juices.

- **Store-bought concentrated natural powders:** These powders, such as the Supernatural brand of colors, are stronger than what you have kicking around in your cupboard and hold their color better in the oven.

- **Activated charcoal powder:** This makes a great dark black color (just use sparingly—a little goes a long way).

Postbaked Dough Color

I try to avoid adding pigment after baking if I can, because you can taste it when it's not been baked, and the crust of the egg wash is pretty impermeable for most pigments anyway. But there is an exception to every rule, and when used sparingly in the following scenarios, you can get a rather nice effect with these pigments:

Luster dusts

- **Luster dusts:** When mixed with a few drops of vodka (or any clear alcohol or extract), luster dust painted on postbake can add a big wow factor. Since you don't want to pile it on, and it is a bit transparent, be mindful of the color you are using underneath. For example, if you want a really bright gold color, try brushing it over a red undercoat. For a more rustic gold, use a brown undercoat. Gold painted over black or white paint looks kind of weird to me, and gold painted over plain pie dough is quite transparent and very subtle.

- **Thin black lines:** Sometimes I will paint thin black-line details postbake, when I need a really crisp line. Tiny handwriting and very thin outlines are good candidates for postbake painting.

- **White touch-ups:** Because opaque colors sometimes crack in the oven, it is necessary to fill in those cracks with a bit more paint (such as opaque white icing color) postbake. Just make sure it has time to fully set and dry before you serve it, or your guests (and their tooth color) won't be very happy with you!

Food Safe Brushes

With food-safe brushes, you can paint on pie dough pretty much like you would any other surface, but only *if* you keep them food-safe. Any natural sable brush or brushes bought at baking-supply stores

Brush ferrule

will do. You just have to thoroughly hand-wash them in warm soapy water and thoroughly dry them by patting them down on paper towels and leaving them to dry there overnight. If you just give them a quick rinse and then stick them back in the jar, bits of moisture will remain and compromise their food safeness. Another important tip for keeping your brushes in good condition is to never dip your brush so that paint goes below the ferrule (the metal thingy). When you dip below the ferrule, paint gets stuck under the metal and that moisture is a breeding ground for bacteria. If you accidentally do this once or twice, just wash your brush extra well afterward. But if it becomes a habit, you'll need to change out your brushes every month to be on the safe side!

Troubleshooting

There are a number of minor nuisances that can de-awesome your pretty paint job. Here are some quick fixes for the most common of these:

- **Feathering:** If your paint is feathering or bleeding out instead of leaving a nice crisp line, first paint your dough surface with a plain emulsifier (vanilla extract or vodka), let it sit a minute, and then gently pat it dry with a clean paper towel. Now you should be able to paint normally without the feathering (see photo at right). If you need to paint very thin

lines (for example, tiny writing), it may be better to paint those on postbake.

- **Flour on the dough surface:** Simply pat the flour off with a damp paper towel, and then let the surface dry before painting.

- **Streaks:** If your paint is streaky, you may need a better emulsifier, like straight-up vodka. It could also be that your ratio of pigment to liquid is too low and your brush is too wet. If that's the case, ease up on the liquid.

- **Cracks:** Sometimes opaque color cracks after you bake it because it sits on the surface of the dough rather than absorbing in like the gel food colors. To deal with this, use opaque icing colors sparingly, limit the bake time on opaque-colored pieces if possible, and, as a last resort, touch up the cracks postbake. I say "last resort" because anything added postbake will be tasteable, and most pigments taste fairly yucky.

- **Colors changing after baking:** The heat of baking causes certain chemical reactions to occur, and enzymatic browning (aka the Maillard reaction) is one of these. Only certain pigments are affected by it, however. If you are working on a special pie and it's important to you that the colors remain true, do a test bake with some scrap dough first to see if the pigments you've chosen will change. You may need to choose what is more important to you—an all-natural pigment or a really vibrant artificial pigment—since, sadly, *natural* and *vibrant* don't usually go together.

Feathering

Working with Paper Templates

You can certainly freehand cut shapes (see Cutting Pie Dough on page 41) out of your pie dough, but as we've discussed, it's all about speed when you're working against the ticking clock of melting butter. Cutting around templates allows you to move quickly, avoid mistakes, and front-load any artsy indecisiveness to the time before your dough is rolled out. While pretty much any nontoxic material that you can cut can be used to make a Pie Art template, such as parchment paper, cardboard, or acetate, plain ol' printer paper is something most of us have kicking around the house, and it's easy to cut. It's also what I used for all the projects in this book.

To make your templates, you can either print them out from your computer or, if you're lazy like me and don't feel like loading the printer, trace them directly off your screen with a dull pencil. You can find out more about this process in the Templates section on page 206. Even though we will only be cutting out the perimeter lines of our templates, I like to draw the inner details on too—both for reference and for a little trick I will share with you below.

Once you've got your template outlined on the paper, go ahead and cut it out. But if it is a particularly detailed design, don't drive yourself nuts trying to cut around every tiny little detail. Remember, you'll

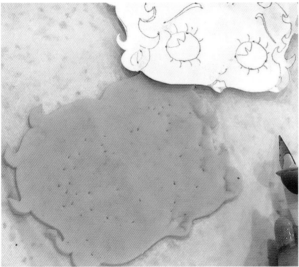

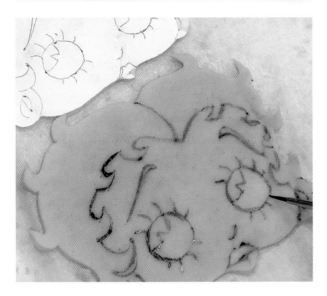

have to cut this out again on the dough! It's okay to simplify details like wavy hair, spokes on gears, text, or other fiddly bits; you can save the detailed cutting for the dough.

Fortunately, working with paper templates is pretty intuitive, but there are several best practices that will help you avoid the few minor annoyances that can pop up:

- Do your cutting when your dough is at its coldest, fresh out of the fridge, and cut the smallest, fiddliest details first.

- Keep your dough relatively dry so that your paper templates don't suck up too much moisture and curl up. If your dough is wet, lightly blot it with a paper towel before you place your stencil.

- Conversely, if your dough is dry and floury, your stencil may slide around on you. If this happens, dab a tiny amount of pasteurized egg whites (see page 28) in a few corners to help it stick.

- Templates only guide us in cutting the exterior contours. To create a guide for the interior contours, use a very, very sharp knife and poke little guide holes through your stencil at key points in the interior design. These will help you correctly paint and sculpt the details once the stencil is removed, and afterward, they will seal up in the oven so no one will ever know they were there. The three photos at the left illustrate this process.

- Paper templates are for one-time use only because of the moisture they absorb. If you want to make the same design multiple times, it may be worth hand-cutting your templates out of acetate or investing in a Cricut cutting machine so that you can create your own reusable food-grade acetate stencils.

- If your dough is starting to warm up and it's getting harder to cut around your template, but you don't want to stop and put it in the freezer for 2 minutes, you can hit it with a quick blast of food-safe freeze spray from about a foot away. However, you may want to reserve such high-tech shenanigans for days when it's reeeeally hot in your kitchen and you reeeeally don't have time to keep chilling your dough!

Sculpting Pie Dough

One of my proudest moments as a Pie Artist was the day I figured out that I could blend layers of pie dough together and sculpt them just like clay if I used an edible emulsifier as a blending medium. This was a game changer for me! It meant I could graduate from simple two-dimensional layers of dough stacked on top of each other to sophisticated sculptural 3-D designs that would hold their shape and not separate in the oven.

As exciting as this discovery was, it took a few more months and a few dozen more pies before I was able to perfect the technique of sculpting pie dough and reach a point in which I could consistently achieve results I was happy with. And now I pass these tips on to you:

1. Not all pie doughs will retain sculpted detail equally. Before you go through all the trouble of planning out a complex design (or executing that design!), do your dough test (see page 23). Find out just how much detail your particular dough will be able to retain postbake, and plan your design accordingly. Remember to use the vanilla wash (see Jessica's Tip on page 45). If you can highlight your sculpted detail with pigment, it's okay if your dough puffs up a little, because you only need the *illusion* of depth and detail to come through postbake.

2. Select the right sculpting tools for your particular design. I am fond of fondant sculpting tools, but toothpicks and your own fingernails can work wonders too!

3. Plan your "depth story." Because pie dough can only really be stacked about three layers thick before we start running the risk of some areas being underbaked in the center, 3-D designs are really only "2½-D." Much like the sculptures on coins or ancient wall friezes, we can only go so

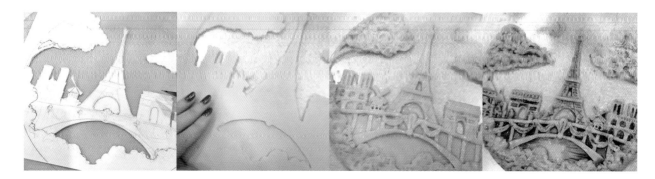

deep. Before you begin, you must decide what parts of your design will be the farthest away, in between, and closest optically. Then you can prepare your templates for these three layers.

4. Now you are ready to cut out the rough layers for your sculpting. If you've got any flour on your dough, lightly blot it away with a slightly damp paper towel. Cut out your template pieces, poke your guide holes through for the interior details, and then paste them together using pasteurized egg whites (see page 28) as the glue. Remember, three layers max!

5. Next, paint the outlines of your interior details lightly with a little brown gel food color mixed with vanilla extract or vodka.

6. Detail time! You may only have three actual layers of depth in your design, but that doesn't mean you can't create the illusion of more depth with a bit of hand-sculpting work. Generously coat the entire dough with pasteurized egg whites to get ready for this step (don't worry if the brown lines bleed a little at this stage).

7. A word about "pushing back" versus "building up" dough. It is far easier to push back, or carve, pie dough than it is to sculpt up. Begin your detail work by first using your sculpting tools to push back the areas meant to appear farther away.

8. As you are pushing back areas, be mindful of dough displacement. The dough you are pushing back has to go somewhere, and not all of it will simply compress into a  denser layer below. If you need to push back large areas of dough, you may need to "scoop it out" so it doesn't smoosh out the side of your design!

9. Once you have finished scoring and pushing back the areas you want to appear farther away, you can finish off the sculpting phase by building up the details meant 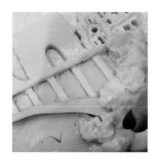 to be on top in your depth story. Use a mini rolling pin to keep the dough for these elements as thin as possible so that your sculpture doesn't get too thick to bake evenly. If any layers still need to be blended together, dunk your fingers in a bit of pasteurized egg whites and hand-smooth the edges down.

10. Once all your sculpting work is done, it's time to lock in the details. Give your project a vanilla wash. Let the pigment seep into the areas meant to be farther away, and leave the areas meant to be closest untouched.

11. Let the vanilla wash set for a bit, and then paint your work however you want or leave it unpainted. Monochrome dough sculptures look really cool too!

12. Chill your work in the freezer while you preheat the oven, and then bake according to your dough test time.

Great job! You're a pie sculptor! Now that you've mastered the hard stuff, let's chillax with a few easy techniques next.

Working with Cutters, Plunger Cutters, and Found Objects

If sculpting pie dough is on the "advanced" side of the Pie Art spectrum, these next techniques are the polar opposite. Even a six-year-old can get fantastic results with them. I know this because my son has been happily using them to make his own Pie Art since he was six!

Cutters, plunger cutters, and found objects are just about the most intuitive tools for making Pie Art. If you can move your arm up and down, you can use these tools. These shapes can either enhance the central figure of your pie design or be the main feature themselves. They are great because they allow you to work fast—no need to sculpt every leaf, flower, or baroque squiggle by painstakingly tracing paper templates if you've got cutters! I mean, you can, but why bother? The only reason you may want to cut out simple shapes like leaves or flowers by hand would be if you (a) don't have a cutter available, or (b) want your shapes to be unique. But, anyway, that's never bothered me. The art is in arranging the shapes nicely, not so much in the uniqueness of the shapes themselves, in my humble opinion!

Depending on how fussy your dough is, you may want to leave the shapes you cut out in place on your parchment paper and remove the excess dough around them, rather than trying to lift the shape. This is a particularly good idea for shapes like stars or letters with sharp edges you want to retain.

Cutters

Cutters

Cutters are any type of plastic- or metal-extruded 2-D shape used to cut out dough. They can be traditional cookie cutters, thicker biscuit cutters, fondant trim cutters (aka impression sticks), or even shapes you make yourself by bending sheet metal or printing plastic on a 3-D printer. To use cutters, simply sprinkle a little bit of flour off to the side, tap your cutter in the flour, and then press the cutter into your dough. Give it a little jiggle and lift up. If the dough shape comes up with your cutter, just poke it with your finger or the end of a paintbrush handle to get it to fall out.

Plunger Cutters

Plunger cutters are another type of cutting tool that create shapes quickly and easily while also giving a little bit of texture to the center of the shape. The plunger cutter has the added bonus of being able to "boot" the dough out if it comes up with the cutter. Plunger cutters are used the same way as regular cutters, with the extra step of depressing the plunger once the shape has been cut to add extra texture.

Plunger cutters

Found Objects

Found object cutters are a neat way of cutting and scoring shapes in your dough without having to fork out any money on new kitchen gadgets. Just make sure you choose items that are food-safe and won't harbor any bacteria or other nasties. A good way to tell if an object is food-safe is whether or not it can safely go in your dishwasher. Most nonporous plastic and metal objects will fit the bill.

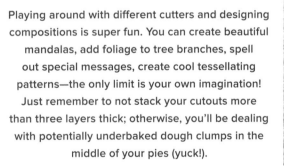

✴ Jessica's Tip ✴

Playing around with different cutters and designing compositions is super fun. You can create beautiful mandalas, add foliage to tree branches, spell out special messages, create cool tessellating patterns—the only limit is your own imagination! Just remember to not stack your cutouts more than three layers thick; otherwise, you'll be dealing with potentially underbaked dough clumps in the middle of your pies (yuck!).

None of the projects in this book require the use of these tools, though sometimes they are given as an "option" if you have any on hand. I wanted to make sure that people could follow these tutorials even if they didn't own a single fancy baking tool. But don't let that stop you from using your own cutters, plunger cutters, and found objects for these projects. I would if I were you!

Found objects

Working with Molds and Impression Mats

Molds and impression mats have been a staple of cake art for decades, but despite their fabulous potential with pastry, it is only in the past couple of years that companies have begun releasing silicone molds designed especially for Pie Art. The good news is that any mold or textured silicone mat intended for use with food can be used with pie dough. There are just a few tricks to ensure the decorations you create with them turn out according to plan!

Just as we discussed in Sculpting Pie Dough on page 50, making sure your particular dough is capable of retaining molded detail is the first step in successfully working with molds. Do a quick dough test with vanilla wash (see ThePieous's Dough Test on page 23 and Jessica's Tip on page 45) using the mold you intend to use for your pie design and see what

happens to one molded piece before you commit to making all your components. Some doughs are better than others at retaining sharp details. But with the exception of puff pastry and rough puff doughs, you should be able to get respectable results from most of the doughs out there by following my tips to overcome three challenges in working with molds.

Various types of molds

A mold in action

Three Challenges in Using Molds

#1: Getting the Dough out of the Mold without Stretching It

One of the biggest mistakes people make when they first try to use silicone molds with pie dough is treating the dough the same way they treat fondant. We know that lifting or stretching pie dough is a big no-no because the stretched-out gluten strands will contract in the oven and cause our dough to shrink in the opposite direction of the stretch. But how do we get the dough out of the molds if we can't lift it out like fondant? Here's how:

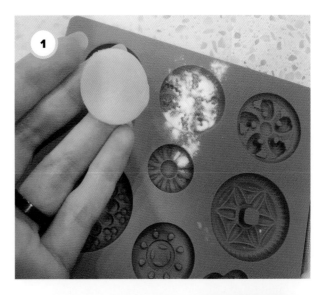

1. Make sure your mold is well floured between each insertion of pie dough. Chill the dough you want to mold for a few minutes in the freezer if you are not working with it straight from the fridge. Warm dough is too mushy to mold.

2. Cut your dough piece as close to the size of the mold shape as you can, and then press it straight down into the mold with your thumb rather than dragging a ball of dough across the mold like fondant. If there is any excess dough, wipe it off to the side while still pressing down and remove it so that you don't pull the soft dough out of the mold.

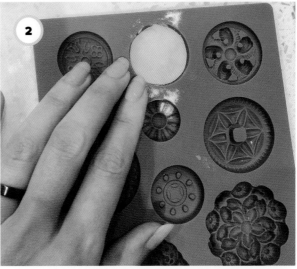

3. Flip the mold upside down, and then *peel the mold itself* up and away from the molded dough piece. You can use a toothpick to encourage it to fall out. Never try to pull the molded dough away from the mold! Doing so will cause it to stretch out, and then it will shrink in the oven. If your dough is not falling out, try sticking the mold with the dough inside in the freezer for 2 minutes, then use more flour for the next piece.

#2: Limiting the Puff of Molded Components in the Oven

When you are finished with your design work, place the entire project into the freezer on your parchment-lined flexible cutting mat while you wait for the oven to heat up. When you are ready, place your work directly into the hot oven from the freezer. Baking frozen designs limits the puff and spread because the outside bakes and locks in the form before the inside has a chance to melt and cause the dough to spread.

#3: Enhancing the Visibility of the Molded Details

Even if you have molded your dough perfectly, and are able to freeze it before baking, you will still want to amp up the definition of those fancy little details with some vanilla wash (see Jessica's Tip on page 45). Letting the mixture seep into the cracks of the sculpture, leaving the higher parts untouched, will help lock in the design.

These are the basics for using standard silicone fondant molds with pie dough, but you may encounter two other molds that require special handling: border molds and impression mats.

Border Molds

Border molds function the same way as other decorative molds, but they require a bit of extra care in handling because of how delicate long strips of dough can be. If your dough is extra fussy, you may want to unmold your border pieces directly onto a stainless-steel ruler or long spatula so that you can easily transfer them over to your pie without breaking them.

It usually takes three or four pieces of molded trim to go all the way around a 9-inch (23 cm) pie. This means you are going to have to contend with seams. Make sure you slightly overlap your trim segments and blend them into one another with a bit of pasteurized egg whites and the back of your fingernail; otherwise, when your pie shrinks in the oven, the trim segments will *not* shrink *as one*, and you'll end up with unsightly gaps in your trim.

Border molds

Impression Mats

Impression mats are basically one really big mold. They're great for adding texture to the background of your pies and come in all sorts of cool designs, like wood grain, honeycomb, damask, and flowers. To get the best results from impression mats, follow these steps:

1. Make sure your mat is well floured, and then flip it on top of your dough.

2. Roll a rolling pin over the back of the mat firmly once *in each direction* so that when the dough shrinks in the oven, it does not shrink in one direction only and distort your design. Even better, instead of rolling, press your mat straight down into your dough with a big book or the bottom of a pie pan.

3. Peel your impression mat up and away from your dough carefully, ensuring that you don't inadvertently lift up your dough with it, causing it to stretch.

4. Give your dough a vanilla wash (see Jessica's Tip on page 45) and let the pigment seep into the cracks of the design so that they remain visible after the dough puffs up in the oven.

Impression mats

That's about all there is to it! Molds and impression mats are a delightful way to add sophisticated detail to your pie designs quickly and easily. I avoided using them for the projects in this book because I know that not everyone has these items kicking around their house, but if you do, by all means use them to spiff up these designs and take them to the next level!

Working with Stencils

I love stencils, and I love using stencils for Pie Art. They're cheap to make and buy, quick to use, easy to master, and they create a big visual impact. They even work on the fussiest, most fragile, and puffiest of doughs. You can make your own custom-designed stencils to create one-of-a-kind patterns and compositions, or even the faces of your friends and favorite celebrities! But you can also nip over to the craft store and pick up all kinds of cool premade stencil designs, like folk art, damask, floral, art deco, geometric, typographic—there are so many options! And if you don't have time to make or buy stencils, you can use random stuff from around your home, like hole punches, bits of ribbon, and lace, to create awesome stencil effects too.

You can certainly just dive into working with stencils and have fun playing around and achieving neat results. All you need to get started are three things:

1. A food-safe stencil

2. An edible adhesive, like pasteurized egg whites (see page 28)

3. An edible powder or pigment to sprinkle or dab through the stencils

But for those of you interested in taking your pie stenciling to the next level and achieving super-crisp professional results, have a read through these Pie Art stenciling best practices.

The two big challenges when it comes to stenciling, on or off pies, is keeping the edges crisp and preventing color from falling onto the non-stenciled areas. Follow the steps on pages 58 and 59 to get perfect stencil results.

Did I mention that I love stencils?

1. Roll out your dough on a parchment-lined flexible cutting mat and cut it into whatever shape you desire for the outer dimensions of your stencil—this could be the size of your pie pan, a smaller medallion shape, or even the profile of someone's face. All dough types work well with stencils, even puff pastry. Prep the surface of your dough by brushing off any excess flour and lightly blotting it with a damp paper towel if needed.

2. Place a small dot of pasteurized egg white on any two corners of your dough to paste your stencil down. Not too much! You don't want to make it difficult to remove your stencil; you just want to keep it from sliding around. Place your stencil.

3. Using a pastry brush or your fingers, dab a small amount of pasteurized egg whites straight down through the stencil holes. Don't paint it on with a wiping motion. Wiping will make some of this "glue" seep under the stencil, which can cause the edges of your stencil design to feather.

4. If you will be stenciling with an edible powder, like cinnamon or activated charcoal, sprinkle the powder over the holes, then tap straight down with your fingers to ensure it is sticking everywhere it needs to be with no gaps. If you are using a pigment like gel food color instead of powder, use a flat, single-use sponge brush to dab your pigment straight down. You don't have to worry about brushing away any excess in the next step.

5. When the powder is tapped in everywhere, carefully brush the excess powder off to the sides of your parchment paper and away from your "clean" dough. Once your stencil is fully covered and any loose powder brushed away, lift your stencil straight up with both hands and immediately away from your work area. Do not peel it diagonally, and do not allow it to tilt because loose powder may fall onto your dough.

6. If any loose powder *does* fall onto your dough, you can carefully scrape it away with a clean sharp knife. You should now have a nice clean stencil image. Carefully brush any loose powder around the outside of your dough completely off the parchment sheet so that it can't contaminate your art surface. Don't sneeze! If you need to move your stenciled dough onto another piece

of dough or onto your pie top, freeze it solid first and then use a cake lifter or spatula to transfer it over.

7. If your stencil is made of food-safe acetate, you can now wash it by hand in warm water, pat it dry with a paper towel, and store it between two paper towels to reuse later.

✶ Jessica's Tip ✶

For those of you who aren't fans of artificial colors, you can really have a blast playing with all sorts of edible powders, like matcha, paprika, cocoa, cinnamon, activated charcoal, butterfly pea flower, and turmeric. You can even layer multiple stencils and use different colors of edible powder or pigment by freezing your dough in between stencil applications. Pie Art silk screen, baby! Try it out, and make your own edible Warhol or art nouveau wallpaper pie. If your friends aren't impressed by that, you need new friends!

Trim Design

Most of the Pie Art techniques I have talked about so far have been in the context of designs for the "middles" of our pies, but what about the edges? The trim that we choose to frame our Pie Art has just as big an impact on its final look and feel as the frame on any valuable painting or photograph. Should the frame be slick and modern? Chunky and rustic? Baroque and fancy? Minimalist? Or the star of the show?

It's up to you to decide what style of trim will suit your pie the best. Just make sure that it is a considered decision and not simply based on what you happen to have always done. There are so many fun options to choose from! And depending on what you choose, there are several ways you'll need to prepare your base pie to get the results you want.

Infinity Edge

Just like an infinity-edge swimming pool, infinity-edge pies have no outer rim of dough poking above the filling—the filling goes right to the edges of the pan. This type of pie trim is used whenever your pie top is designed to go right to the edges of the pan. The filling itself acts as a glue to bind the top decoration to the base pie and fuse the two together. Just make sure that you bake infinity-edge pies on a parchment-lined baking sheet! The filling is very likely to bubble up and over your pan, given the absence of a raised trim. But don't worry—it will sink back down once it cools. Use a wet butter knife to clean up any messes as soon as your pie comes out of the oven, and then place your cooled top decoration with a cake lifter before the filling has a chance to set.

Crimped Edge

There are sooo many classic crimped-edge pie designs, and new ones are being invented every

Infinity edge

Crimped edge

day! To create a crimped-edge pie, simply cut your pie dough circle a few inches wider than your pan, fold over the excess to form a little vertical "dough wall," and then poke at it using your fingers, utensils, stamps, or any number of the zillion crimping techniques available. I have links to many edge-crimping tutorials in the Resources section on page 228, so don't feel obliged to stick with the simple one I present in this book. Choose your favorite and make it your own!

You can use crimped-edge trims anytime your top decoration does not extend all the way to the edges of the pie and floats in the center like a medallion or anytime your top decoration is going to be baked directly on the base pie. In the latter case, the top decoration can be folded over into the dough being raised for crimping.

Braids, Twists, and Molded Trim

Preparing your base pie for the addition of braids, twists, and molded trim pieces is similar to preparing an infinity-edge pie, except you don't quite draw the filling all the way over the top of the edges. I provide links to several braid and twist tutorials in the Resources section on page 228, and you can refer to the Working with Molds and Impression Mats section on page 54 for guidance on preparing molded trim pieces. You will usually have to create three or four segments of this type of trim, depending on how large your pie is. Overlap your pieces slightly and connect them together with a bit of pasteurized egg whites (see page 28) by dragging some dough from one piece into the neighboring piece with the back of your fingernail. If you forget this step, your trim pieces may separate from one another when the dough shrinks in the oven, leaving fuggly gaps.

Appliqués

Trim designs composed of dough appliqués take up a bit of extra real estate on your pie, but they can be quite charming! You can layer simple geometric cutouts like circles, create fancy floral wreaths with plunger cutters, or get really elaborate by weaving hand-cut vines around little berries, nuts, or other edible decorations. There are two ways you can accomplish this look:

1. Bake your dough appliqués separately on a baking sheet. Then create a base pie with an infinity edge. The moment the base pie comes out of the oven, place your now-cooled cutout pieces onto the edges of the pie. The hot filling will fuse them to the pie as it cools and sets. If, for any reason, you forget to place your appliqués

Braided edge

Appliqué

on while the filling is still hot, you'll need to attach them with some sort of edible adhesive. This could be sugar glue, an extra bit of filling, toasted marshmallow or meringue, melted chocolate, icing, or melted cheese in the case of savory pies!

2. Bake your appliqués directly onto the base pie. This is slightly more challenging than the previous method because the parts of the appliqués not touching the filling will bake faster than the parts that are in contact with moisture. You'll need to cover the edges with aluminum foil for most of the bake and remove the foil only for the last 10 to 15 minutes. You also have to worry about gravity pulling on any part of the appliqués' dough that is hanging over the edge of your pie pan. If you have leaves or other elements that you would like to have sticking out over the side, but you don't want to add them postbake, you'll need to create a little foil "shelf" for them to rest on. You can do this by balling up or folding over some aluminum foil on a baking sheet and tucking it under the areas you are concerned might get droopy.

Appliqués applied postbake

Appliqués baked directly onto the base pie (with a foil "shelf")

★ **Jessica's Tip** ★

Honorable mention for trim designs that don't incorporate any dough at all! With an infinity-edge design, you can sprinkle on crushed cookies, pretzels, mini marshmallows, chocolate sprinkles, toasted nuts, or any number of lovely and delicious little doodads. Just make sure to add these elements shortly before serving your pie, as many of them, like pretzels and toasted nuts, do not hold up well when they absorb moisture in the fridge.

Putting It All Together

One of the biggest challenges aspiring Pie Artists face when trying to bake beautiful pies that taste great is ensuring that all the different components of their pie—the filling, the bottom crust, the top decorations of various thicknesses—bake correctly. It seems that one component is always trying to sabotage the others. If you bake the pie long enough for the bottom crust to be done properly, the top decorations get burned. If you take the pie out when the top decorations are perfectly golden brown, the bottom is still soggy and the filling not yet set. And if you take the time to tent the top decorations in foil so that they don't burn while the bottom crust is baking, the filling explodes all over the place and ruins your design. Arrgghh!

It is absolutely true that the bottom crust and filling for most pies need more time to properly bake than the top decorations. And, to date, the conventional wisdom has dictated covering the pie top and edges in foil to shield these bits from the heat. But there are three problems with this:

1. It doesn't always stop the top from getting overbaked before the bottom is done.

2. It doesn't stop the filling from exploding over the top of the pie.

3. It's a pain in the butt!

I'll let you in on a little secret I learned very early in my pie-making career: there is no reason for all the components of your pie to be baked together!

At least not for the entire bake time. For the majority of my pies, the base pie and the top decorations are baked separately, and then

combined postbake. Folks' first question on hearing this is usually, "Doesn't the top fall off when you go to cut and serve the pie?" And the answer is "Nope!" Here's why.

Assembling Your Prebaked Pie Components

Assembling prebaked pie components is very easy and results in one cohesive, fused-together pie at the end when you follow this simple method:

1. Bake your top decorations on a parchment-lined baking sheet, and then allow them to cool.

2. Go ahead and bake your base pie according to your recipe.

3. Get your oven mitts, cake lifter, and top decorations near the oven and ready to go.

4. The moment you take your base pie out of the oven and it is still bubbling hot, carefully lift your top decorations off the baking sheet with the cake lifter and place them onto the base pie.

1. Precook your filling in a pot on the stove so that it has a chance to boil and get to its setting temperature. Once it has boiled, throw in a handful or two of raw fruit. The raw fruit in the precooked filling will ensure that the texture/mouthfeel of the pie is appealing, without running the risk of exploding all over your pretty lattice or cutouts. Set the filling aside to cool (you don't want to add hot filling to a pie shell—instant mush!).

2. Assemble your pie dough in its pan and par-bake your pie shell for 15 minutes. Because your filling is precooked, your pie won't need to be in the oven as long as it otherwise would need to be. This means that the base pie won't have quite enough time to fully cook unless you also prebake the dough shell on its own first too (I told you it was a little involved!). Refer to page 226 and the Resources section on page 228 for detailed instructions on how to par-bake a pie shell, but in a nutshell, you just have to put the rolled dough into the pie pan, line it with parchment, pour in pie weights (ceramic balls, rice, sugar, beans), and bake it for 10 to 15 minutes.

5. Gently press down on the top with your hands or oven mitts for about 5 to 10 seconds to form the seal.

Congrats! Now your top and bottom are fused together as one, and as soon as the filling has set, you will be able to cut and serve your pie just the same as if they were always baked together. If you have ever let pie filling cool on a pan or server and tried to scrub it off later, you know that stuff basically becomes superglue once it's set, so that pie top is not going anywhere.

What about Domed Pies?

On some rare occasions, you just can't avoid baking the top decoration with the base pie—for instance, when making a domed mile-high apple pie or when you want to integrate a lattice into a crimped edge. However, you can still keep your pies from going "rustic" and exploding on you when the filling boils in the oven. Fair warning, though: It is a little involved, so you really have to care about keeping your pie top clean!

3. After you have prebaked your shell and precooked your filling, you can add the cooled filling into the shell and then add the top layer of dough. Cover the edges with foil and bake according to your usual recipe, minus 10 or 15 minutes. Remove the foil when 10 minutes is left in the bake.

As I said, you have to reaaaally want to keep your pie pristine-looking to go to all this trouble. If you can't get away with only baking the top and bottom separately, it's probably better to just be at peace with a few fruity explosions here or there. Heck, I'll still eat it!

Other Assembly Considerations

So we know that the top, filling, and bottom of our pies have their own special needs, but what about those other decorations we sometimes want to add to our Pie Art designs? They have their preferred times and methods of being introduced to the party too. Fortunately, it's all pretty intuitive!

Do You Want It to Melt?
Shredded cheese, brûlée sugar, marshmallows—some additions benefit from the ambient heat of the pie and should be added right after the pie is removed from the oven.

Do You Want It NOT to Melt?
Fancy sugar work, chocolate ornaments, whipped toppings—some ingredients just hate getting all hot and sweaty and should only be added after the pie has fully cooled.

Do You Need to Keep It Dry?
Roasted nuts, crushed pretzels, wafer-paper decorations—these elements despise moisture and go all gummy and bendy when they absorb it, so make sure to add them after the pie has stopped steaming and don't put them in the fridge!

Do You Have Top Decorations That Are More Than Three Layers of Dough Thick?
Bake those elements separately from the rest of your top decoration, and then glue them on at the assembly stage with some edible adhesive (see page 28). These might be elements like dough bows, thick dough roses, or little balls of dough. If you try to bake them on your top crust, they are very likely to be underbaked and gummy in the middle, which is gross.

Do You Need to Attach Things after the Pie Has Already Cooled?
If you need to glue any broken pieces or extra decorations onto your pie after it has cooled, try melted marshmallow, melted isomalt, melted chocolate, melted cheese, sugar glue, jam, excess pie filling, or royal icing. Just remember that people have to eat this, so choose a "glue" that will complement the flavor of your pie!

Do You Not Have Time for Any of This?
If you can't wait for things to cool down or if your edible glue is not setting fast enough, whip out the secret pie-assembly weapon: food-safe freeze spray. Just make sure you choose a food-safe freeze spray, like the kind used for sensitive electronics, and not an automotive freeze spray that gets poisonous residue on everything!

✦ Jessica's Tip ✦
Never try to lift dough decorations or, worse, entire top crusts when they are still hot. Hot pastry is very fragile and even with a *full-size cake lifter*, they will crack under the slightest pressure.

Now that you know the big secret behind creating perfectly baked pies that taste as good as they look, we're ready to explore some "avant-garde" pie-assembly tricks.

Taking Your Pies Higher

The pies we talk about in the Putting It All Together section on page 63 are your standard, everyday flat-circle-on-a-table sort of pies. But what if you want to assemble some pies that are a little more ambitious? Pies with some "loftier aspirations," as it were? Perhaps even venture into Piescraper territory? Read on.

One of the major reasons why pies have been losing out in the big "pie versus cake" debate at weddings and major events is that they lack oomph on the buffet table. A flat little circle of pastry just can't compete with stacks of cake tiers for that across-the-room wow factor, no matter how delicious it is. But what if there were a way to help our vertically challenged little pastry friend gain some stature, and reclaim its rightful place in the buffet table spotlight?

The good news is, there is! We just need to equip our pies with a few supports to help them reach these new heights.

A standee being attached for support

Standees

One way of introducing some verticality to your pie is by adding dough *standees* to the top. "Standees" is my term for cutout vertical panels of dough supported by little right-angle dough triangles hidden in the back and attached with edible adhesive (see page 28). If you've ever seen a cardboard cutout of your fave celeb at the movie theater or a cardboard corporate mascot in a mall, you get the concept!

Standees obviously have a "back" that isn't meant to be viewed, but for pies destined for buffet tables placed against a wall, this is no biggie.

Your standee topper can be anything from a simple geometric shape, like a heart with initials, or as complex as the painstakingly sculpted entire cast of your favorite cartoon series. And if you're feeling "extra," and you want your pie to be viewed from all sides, you can

make your standees double-sided, too, by cutting out mirror-image shapes and pasting them together.

Now it is true that some doughs naturally have no problem "going vertical"—cookie-type doughs and hot-water crusts, for instance—but most types of pie dough will need a little more assistance than just a triangular support prop in back. That is where my "double-dough" method comes in!

The Double-Dough Method

Basic shortcrust pastry is too thin and flaky to support its own weight when standing up in a pie filling; however, two layers of that same pastry, glued together with a strong moisture barrier adhesive, have no problem doing so. When I want to create a standee for one of my pies using pastry, I prepare a double layer of dough by placing down a ⅛-inch (3 mm) layer of pie dough, coating it with whole egg wash or jam, layering a second ⅛-inch (3 mm) layer of pie dough on top of it, patting them together with my hands, and then cutting out my shape and painting as usual. Preparing the dough this way accomplishes two things: one, it makes the dough panel sturdier and capable of supporting its own weight to a height of up to 6 inches (15 cm), and two, it creates a moisture barrier so that if the dough panel is sitting below the filling line for a long time, it won't get all bendy and break off.

When placing your standee into your base pie, simply cut two slots in the filling perpendicular to

Preparing a double layer of dough

A standee with the double-dough method

each other—one for the front panel and one for the support prop—and then gently nudge your standee into place. Easy peasy!

Its super fun creating cool-looking standee decorations for pies, but we want them to contribute to the fun of eating the pie too. My family likes to break standees off and use them as "pie nachos" to scoop up the filling (and we say "Arrrgghhh!" when we bite their little dough heads off, of course). You can also coat the backs of your standees in jam, chocolate, or cheese to make them delicious little snacks in their own right.

Tall Pie Pans

While creating standee toppers for traditional flat pies is a great way to add some height and fun, they can only take us about 6 inches (15 cm) high before they run the risk of keeling over. So how can we take things even higher? Well, for certain types of dough—ones capable of supporting their own weight outside of the pan—the pan itself can provide the initial support needed. Italian pasta frolla tarts are famous for their silicone embossed vertical trim decorations, and hot-water crust pies have been molded high in tall, sculpted springform pie tins for centuries. You can also create your own forms and molds for pies made with this sort of sturdy dough by repurposing silicone cake molds or metal cake pans or by cutting and reshaping disposable aluminum pie pans.

Experiment and see what new shapes and heights you can reach with different materials.

Armatures

All right, standees, freestanding tall pies, check, check. But that still doesn't get us to "epic." That still doesn't get us to "Wow, look at that amazing towering pie on that buffet table across the room!" For this level of impact, we're going to need a little more support in the form of armatures.

Epic multitiered cakes all have armatures to support their weight too. There's no shame in artfully incorporating a few nonfood props, provided they are food-safe and don't interfere with our ability to actually eat the pie!

Steel Spools

A creation with steel-spool armature

My go-to armature for my signature multitiered wedding Piescrapers are stainless-steel sanitary spools.

They are dishwasher-safe, sturdy, and reusable. I provide links to places where you can buy these in the Resources section on page 228, but you should be able to find them in most plumbing-supply stores. They are just wide enough to safely support

Steel spools in action

a standard 9-inch (23 cm) pie pan, but small enough to easily conceal behind vertical dough panels.

I typically use melted chocolate or royal icing to temporarily glue these spools to the bottom of tart pans to act as my Piescraper armature. The wedding Piescraper project on page 199 is dedicated to working with these spools, but they are pretty intuitive. Just make sure that you assemble your Piescrapers in place at the venue—don't try to travel with a fully assembled Piescraper in your car!

Custom Wire Armature

The steel spool and tart bottom combo is pretty great for supporting towering multitiered Piescrapers, but sometimes we have something a little different in mind, and we need a more customized kind of support. That's when food-safe steel wire becomes a godsend!

For the tree Piescraper in the photo below, I wanted it to appear as if three tarts were floating above the main pie. I created little loops of wire to hold the tarts and hid the supports behind the main tree. Had I been making this pie for an event where people might see the back, I would also have covered up the wires in the back with another panel of dough, but you get the idea.

A creation with custom wire armature

The sky's the limit when it comes to the heights you can take your Pie Art designs to, and any way you slice it, things are looking up!

Displaying Your Pie Art

I've just talked about some ways to get your pies to stand out on the dessert table by making them three-dimensional, but how do you make your two-dimensional pie designs stand out at the party too? After all, you've spent far too many hours toiling over that gorgeous work of Pie Art to simply plunk it in the middle of the table like some lowly potato casserole!

Well, we may not have a three-dimensional piece of Pie Art to work with, but we can certainly make our "frame" for that artwork three-dimensional! Here are some fun ways to pay proper respect to traditional flat pies when presenting them to guests.

Dessert Stands

The first order of business is to elevate that pie above the rest of the common table denizens—figuratively and literally! Choose a dessert stand that complements the style of your pie as well as the theme of the event. Is it a rustic pie? Try a wooden stand or natural-glaze ceramic stand. Are you having a proper tea and crumpets sort of affair? Go for a porcelain or glass stand. Something a little more modern and slick? How about a unique metal stand?

If you're feeling really artsy, and this pie is going to be the centerpiece of something beyond a simple dinner party, get creative with your stand too! Try a stack of old leather books, glass blocks with fairy lights, or an old tree stump. The only limit is your imagination. Whatever you choose, jacking that pie up is the first step in claiming the spotlight.

Trim Rings

If your pie is made with the kind of dough that can hold itself up outside of the pan, great! It'll look fabulous on its dessert stand solo or on a simple napkin or doily. But if you are working with a traditional shortcrust pie, you're going to be stuck looking at the side of some sort of pie pan. If, like me, you prefer baking in metal pans for the heat conduction, but you hate the look, here are a couple of ways you can disguise your unsophisticated pan sides.

Put the Whole Thing into a Larger, Prettier Ceramic Pan
No one needs to know it wasn't baked in that lovely fluted, chunky antique pie plate! This is an especially great cheat for pie baked in disposable pie tins.

Dessert stands

A ceramic pan as a trim ring

If the metal rim is peeking out conspicuously, you can always disguise the edges with a quick application of some whipped cream, crushed nuts, sprinkles, or sliced fruits.

Slip a Band of Cardboard and Ribbon around the Metal Edge

This is my go-to, and I keep an assortment of these homemade bands around for this purpose. Ribbon alone likely won't be good enough because your pie pan is probably slanted in and there will be nothing for the ribbon to attach to. But if you staple or hot-glue your ribbon to a strip of black cardstock of the same size, it will stand up nicely. You can match the ribbon to your party decor!

Decorative elements as a trim ring

A ribbon band as a trim ring

Hide the Pan Edges with Flowers, Fruits, or Other Decorative Elements

You'll need a dessert stand that is wider than your pie pan for this, but it's pretty straightforward. Just pile a collection of pretty things all the way around your pie to take attention away from the boring sides. But make sure you don't surround your pie with anything dangerous, like poisonous flowers or leaves!

Complementary Decor

Once you've given your pie some height and dealt with the sides of the pan, it's time to think about the larger mise-en-scène. How are you going to tie your pie in with the rest of the table decor?

Place a runner or fabric swag under the pie stand, and add some fresh flowers, fruit, sequins, or styling props around the base. There are plenty of inspiring examples of table decor that you can draw from online. Feel free to get really creative with this! If all your lovely table decor is emanating from the pie in the center on a raised pedestal, it doesn't matter whether your Pie Art is flat—it's still going to be the prettiest girl at the dance.

Complementary decor

Troubleshooting

Ahhh, my favorite section, Troubleshooting.

Because at its heart, Pie Art is about experimentation and creative expression, things are . . . well, they are invariably going to go sideways on you at some point. But does that mean you have to scrap the whole endeavor and show up to the party empty-handed? No!

My followers were kind enough to send me a list of their "most common pie fails" (thanks, y'all!). Just have a skim through and find your problem along with the solution that'll turn those lemons into lemon pie!

Your Dough Is Sticking to Your Work Surface

So you've added too much water and made a batch of dough that's too sticky. You're late, out of ingredients, or out of patience, and you just don't have the time or inclination to redo it. You've tried adding some extra flour to your work surface already, but the dough is still sticking to everything. The bad news is that anytime you try to lift a shape you've cut out, it's going to get stuck, tearing and deforming your carefully cutout details. The good news is, you don't have to lift it! While you can't make a braid or molded pieces easily with overly sticky dough, you can still use cookie cutters and hand-cut shapes. You just have to leave them in place where you cut them, and instead remove the surrounding dough. Then you can freeze them solid, pop a spatula underneath, and now move them with ease! Your final baked pie will be a little tough, but enh, nobody ever died from slightly tough dough.

Your Dough Is Cracking as You Try to Roll It or Braid with It

If your dough is cracking on you, it is possible that it's just a little bit too cold. That's an easy fix, just leave it alone for 10 minutes on the counter and try again. But if you know your dough is the right temperature and it's still cracking on you, it's probably just too dry. You can try adding a little bit of water to patch the cracks back together, but if you're dealing with major cracking, you probably didn't add quite enough fat to your recipe. You can still use it though! Same drill as with our "too sticky" dough: don't try to create braids and weaves, but stick with cutout shapes frozen solid for your decorations. And don't forget to give them a generous coating of pasteurized egg whites (see page 28) to prevent splitting in the oven.

Your Dough Is Too Sticky AND Crumbling Apart!

This is always a fun one. Overly sticky dough means there is too much water. Cracky, crumbly dough means too much flour. Sticky *and* crumbly dough means too much fat. You need those gluten bonds between the flour and water to help hold things together when making braids or weaving dough, and when there are not enough of them, you won't be able to make any decorations that require "pliability" from your dough. Fortunately, in this instance, you actually can salvage your dough! Just break the dough up into little chunks in a cold bowl, sprinkle on a couple tablespoons of extra flour and a teaspoon of water, reblend the whole mixture by "fluffing" it all up (gently tossing it with your hands), and smoosh the balls of dough coated in the flour and water between your fingers quickly. Then bring it together in a ball, flatten into a disk, and rechill. Try rolling it out again in 2 hours. It may end up being slightly too sticky or crumbly or all of the above since you're eyeballing the amount of flour and water to add, but it'll be easier to work with than it was before.

Your Dough Is Puffing Up Too Much in the Oven and Obliterating Your Decorations' Details

Some doughs are just naturally puffy. If it is really important to you to have super-crisp details in your decorations, you should consider choosing a dough designed for that (see ThePieous's Dough Comparison Chart on page 18). But if you just haaaaave to use Grandma's special double-butter rough puff secret family dough recipe, and you just haaaaave to have detailed decorations on top, I can help you out a little. First off, make sure any embossed or sculpted details are given a vanilla wash (see Jessica's Tip on page 45), or are directly painted on, to help define those lines. Second, when you are done making your decorations, put them in the freezer for an hour. Lastly, place them directly from the freezer into a "hotter-than-usual" oven—say, about 425°F (220°C; gas mark 7)—to start. This will help the outer layer of dough cook faster than the inner layer, which limits spread. Just remember to either turn the temperature down after 10 minutes, or reduce your bake time accordingly. Your decorations will still puff up, but they won't be completely obliterated.

Your Dough Is Too Gummy to Cut

Gummy, sticky dough can be a pain in the butt to cut, but it's not impossible! Stick it in the freezer so that it is nice and cold, give the top a very light coating of flour to absorb some of the moisture causing it to stick to the blade of your knife, and then refer to the Press, Don't Pull technique for cutting pie dough on page 42. It'll take longer to cut because you'll have to press straight up and down for every cut, and you'll have to keep rechilling your dough, but you'll get those shapes cut out in the end!

You Forgot to Put a Sheet of Parchment Paper on Top of Your Cutting Mat, and Now You Can't Get the Dough onto the Baking Sheet

This one's easy! Just freeze the dough solid on its cutting mat and then pick it up with a cake lifter and move it over to the baking tray.

Your Paint Is Feathering

If your paint is feathering or bleeding out, it's likely that your dough is too warm or has a bit too much fat in it. Not to worry! Just give the surface of your dough a wash with pasteurized egg whites (see page 28), carefully blot it dry with a paper towel, and let it sit for a minute. This creates a new sealed surface for your pigment to sit on top of and you should be able to get much crisper lines.

A Big Air Bubble Formed in the Middle of Your Pie Art in the Oven

It's not uncommon for large bubbles of air to get trapped beneath layers of pie dough. This is especially true when you are working with multiple layers of dough in projects like Pietraits. The last thing you need on your best friend's portrait that you spent hours making is a big ol' air bubble goiter! Fortunately for you, there is an easy way to deal with these air bubbles, *if* you move fast. When you first take your pie out of the oven, the dough will remain soft and pliable for about 5 seconds before the shock of the cold air hardens the outer layer and locks in the shape forever. During these 5 seconds, if you take your oven mitt and press gently down on the air bubble, and hold it there for 10 seconds, you will be able to successfully squeeze the air out and flatten your pie.

You Made Part of the Top Decoration Too Thick and Now It's Underbaked

If most of your top decoration is underbaked, but a few areas are already done, just cover those parts of the design with foil and continue baking until the rest of the dough is finished. If it's the other way around and most of your top is fully baked, but one or two decorations are not yet finished, that's a bit trickier. You can try to tent the entire design in foil and just cut out a little hole for the area that's underdone, or if you have a kitchen torch handy, you can always try to "spot heat" the raw areas. Keep in mind, however, that this will cook the outer layer of the dough first, so you need to keep your distance to avoid scorching it. Also remember that parchment paper will catch fire if exposed to an open flame, so have your fire-suppression supplies handy!

You Set Your Kitchen on Fire Using a Torch Near Parchment Paper

Step 1: Go back in time and read the part above about parchment paper being combustible around open flames. Step 2: Buy a fire blanket and a Class B/C fire extinguisher and keep them handy in your kitchen at all times.

The Dome of Your Double-Crust Pie Cracked or Completely Collapsed

Easy! Whip up some cutout dough flowers with a cookie cutter and some store-bought dough, bake them for 8 to 10 minutes at 400°F (205°C; gas mark 6), and then use jam to glue them over the crack (or the entire top area if it was a major collapse). Or just accept the cracks, call it "wabi sabi," and throw some edible gold leaf or paint down. Bam! Art.

The Person You Are Baking for Just Told You That They Can't Have Artificial Food Color

As convenient and pretty as artificial colors are, let's face it, they are . . . well, artificial. If you have time to plan ahead, you can order some natural food colors from companies that manufacture them. But if you're going to have to make do with what you've got in the kitchen, you can whip up the following colors at home:

- **Black:** Activated charcoal powder
- **Yellow:** Turmeric powder
- **Orange:** Paprika
- **Pink:** Beet juice
- **Red:** Paprika and beet juice mixed together
- **Mossy green:** Matcha powder
- **Dark green:** Pureed raw spinach
- **Purple:** Mashed blueberries or blackberries
- **Brown:** Ground cinnamon, nutmeg, coffee, or cocoa powder
- **Blue:** Butterfly pea flower powder

Okay, that last one you probably don't have in the house, but most hippie grocery stores do! These colors will dull a little in the oven, and you may get a tinnnnny bit of the taste coming through, but not too much.

The Bottom of Your Crust Is Soggy, but the Top Is Perfect

It is best to always bake the base pie separate from the top decorations if you can. That way they both get to bake exactly the right amount of time for them. But if you have to bake them together, and the bottom crust keeps getting soggy, try blind-baking or par-baking the bottom crust for a bit before you put the filling in. Check out page 226 and the Resources section on page 228 for detailed instructions on blind baking and par-baking.

The Bottom Crust Is Perfect, but the Top Decorations Burned

Next time, cover your decorations with foil, and just remove it for the last 5 to 10 minutes of the bake. That should keep them from getting too crispy. Also try moving your pie lower in the oven.

The Top Decorations Keep Falling Off the Sides in the Oven

There are two solutions for this: either bake them separately and glue them onto the edges postbake with your choice of edible adhesive (see page 28) or create a little support shelf for them out of aluminum foil. You may need to slip some parchment paper in between your foil shelf and the pie dough, however, because foil can sometimes stick to baked dough.

The House Is Too Hot to Work with My Dough, Even after Repeatedly Putting It in the Freezer

If it's just not happening with your dough no matter what you do because of the heat, you gotta swap out your dough. Opt for a dough that doesn't mind being warm, such as hot-water crust or certain cookie doughs, or make a completely different type of pie that doesn't involve pastry at all, like an icebox pie with a graham cracker crust. Then make your top decorations out of fruit, wafer paper, or chocolates, or create a mosaic with nuts and cookie bits.

You Followed the Recipe but You're Getting Different Results Than Everyone Else

Sometimes recipes are just flawed. It happens. But what about those times when everyone else in your circle is getting great results from a recipe, but it just isn't working for you? Altitude, humidity, and oven quirks can all be factors that affect your bake, but it could also be that your measurements are off. Did you know that "1 cup of flour" can be one-quarter more or less than the original baker was using, all depending on how tightly packed the flour is? That's why I **always** go by weight rather than volume when measuring out ingredients. Get yourself a cheap little kitchen scale and say bye-bye to imperfect ingredient measurements!

Just Everything Has Gone Wrong

When everything goes wrong, one word: parfait.

Did all your decorations burn to a crisp? Did you fumble the pie and drop it facedown on your (clean) counter? Is your filling lovely, but the bottom a soggy mess? Don't despair—deconstruct! Here's how to turn your epic pie fail into a delightful pie parfait!

Scoop out the "good bits," whether that is the top decorations, the filling, or the bottom crust, and set them aside in separate bowls. Then get out a set of really pretty champagne flutes or small wineglasses. Crumble your crust and sprinkle a thin layer at the bottom of each glass. Then add a scoop of your filling on top. Continue alternating layers of crumbled piecrust and filling until it is all used up. If you have no workable crust because it is all soggy or burned, crumble graham crackers or whatever cookie you

have on hand that will go well with your filling. Now create a decorative topping for the upper layer. If you happened to make some extra dough flowers, you can always pop those on top, but if not, no biggie. Do you have time to dash to the store on the way to the party and grab a can of whipped topping? If so, perfect! Spray it on in the car and throw down some sprinkles. No one is going to turn their nose up at the beautiful, unique, and appetizing "pie parfaits." They'll probably be asking you for the recipe (that is, if you don't tell them that you actually dropped the pie on the counter first).

Got a problem that we didn't cover here? Then come on over to my Instagram, @thepieous, and leave your question as a comment on one of my posts, or head over to any of the Facebook pie groups and ask the community. You'll have your pick of solutions in no time. Little fails and frustrations are inevitable in the world of pie baking, but the more you fail, the more you learn, and before you know it, you'll be the one doling out all the answers!

A pie parfait

Planning Your Pie Art Designs and Finding Inspiration

Ready to jump in and start creating your own Pie Art designs, but looking for a little more ins-pie-ration to get you started? I've got you covered!

The first part is the easy part: setting your "pie goals." Why are you baking this pie? Do you just want to try out a few new techniques on a pie you plan to eat alone after dinner? Are you hoping to post photos of this pie online and have them go viral, catapulting you and your business to baking stardom? Or are you simply baking this pie to cheer up a dear friend, and your only goal is to make them smile?

Or maybe a little of all three?

Whatever your reason, once you know it, you'll have a metric by which you can judge the success of your pie. Armed with this info, the next step is to start coming up with concept sketches (napkin scribbles are fine!) or written-out ideas that you'll gauge against **four special metrics**. These four metrics constitute the Pie Art trifecta (quadfecta?), virtually guaranteed to result in a successful finished product.

The Four Pie Art Design Metrics

If you can come up with a design that ticks all four boxes—or at least the first three—you are very likely to create a pie that achieves your goals! Now let's take a look at each of these metrics:

1. Your pie looks like real food that someone would actually want to eat.

2. Your pie is an attractive visual composition, independent of the fact that it is a pie.

3. Your pie evokes an emotional response (like humor, warmth, nostalgia) in its intended recipient.

4. Bonus: Your pie involves a simple but novel technique that will inspire replication from others.

The first one might seem obvious, but you'd be surprised by how often people forget the fact that they are working with food that someone has to eat when the design muse takes them! What makes a pie visually appetizing? Flaky golden crusts, glittering jewel-like fruit filling, fluffy mounds of meringue. There are all sorts of visual cues that let us know that what we are about to bite into is going to make our mouths happy. But you can inadvertently obliterate all the "deliciousness cues" with your design if you aren't careful! This is why, in my designs, I try to always leave at least some part of the crust unpainted and always show some of the filling below. Yes, I could just plunk a circle of dough down and paint the Mona Lisa on top, but is anyone going to want to eat that? If, however, I designed an ornate "natural-dough" frame for that painting, cut out a few of the shrubs in the background so that the filling showed through, and maybe slapped down a few whipped cream clouds or chocolate birds, now we're getting those deliciousness cues back and creating a pie that people will want to eat!

The second metric, creating an attractive composition, has to do with using each element of our circular canvas to its fullest, and having them all work together in harmony. Your visual composition usually comprises the following five elements:

1. Central image
2. Background
3. Ornaments
4. Trim
5. Filling

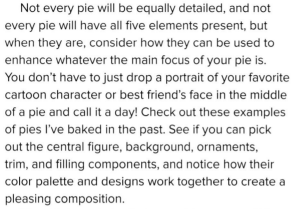

Some of Jessica's Pie Art designs

Not every pie will be equally detailed, and not every pie will have all five elements present, but when they are, consider how they can be used to enhance whatever the main focus of your pie is. You don't have to just drop a portrait of your favorite cartoon character or best friend's face in the middle of a pie and call it a day! Check out these examples of pies I've baked in the past. See if you can pick out the central figure, background, ornaments, trim, and filling components, and notice how their color palette and designs work together to create a pleasing composition.

The third metric is all about subject matter. What pie subject is going to make your audience say "OMG, I LOVE this!" and share the photos with their friends immediately? If the design is for a friend, you can select a character or subject that they love or an inside joke the two of you share. For the general public, you can choose something topical, perhaps connected to a trending meme or TV show. If you're trying to attract the notice of press, you could choose subjects that are connected to what they will be writing about next, like upcoming holidays or global events. Or you could just tap into your favorite cultural zeitgeist with a little timeless nostalgia—the roaring twenties, hippie sixties, retro future, Victorian steampunk, and so on. Whether you go the "broad social appeal" route or the "ultra-niche" route, you're bound to strike a chord with someone!

The fourth and final metric is listed as "bonus" because it's not easy to pull off, but when you can, daaayyymmn! To accomplish the fourth goal, you have to invent a new baking technique, which no one has ever seen before (at least not in modern memory), that is super attractive *and* compelling, and is simple enough that anyone looking at it will think to themself, "I bet I could make that!"

Simple yet unique and compelling concepts are surprisingly difficult to pull off in any industry, but that shouldn't stop you from trying! If you can hit upon a signature style that ticks these boxes, that's pretty much a guarantee that you and your work will go viral. And if you can do it more than once, you can parlay those 15 minutes of fame into a real artsy baking career!

Where to Find Visual Inspiration

It's great that we now know *what* we want to make in broad terms, but where do we go to find inspiration for what it could actually look like?

A rule of thumb for established and aspiring artists looking for inspiration is to *not* start with looking at other examples of the item you are about to make. If you are designing a new wedding dress, don't start by looking at other wedding dresses. If you are designing a fancy cake, don't start by looking at other fancy cakes. Why?

Most inspiration strikes when we are thinking about the juxtaposition between two completely different things.

Some of Jessica's Pie Art designs

A dress and a tree. A cake and a crystal mine. A pie and a classical architecture facade. A concept car and a piece of music. A floral centerpiece and a clock. You get the idea. Looking at other people's Pie Art is a great way to reverse-engineer techniques and learn about what's possible, but if you are looking for truly new and unique ideas, you'll want to get your inspiration from outside of the baking realm.

These are some of my favorite topics to browse whenever I'm stuck for ideas. You can make a sort of Mad Libs game of it! Pick any two topics, and then brainstorm ways you could make a pie, borrowing techniques and subject matter from those two things:

- **Fine art:** Art deco, pop art, children's art

- **Nature:** Animals, tree branches, cloud formations

- **Fashion:** Haute couture dresses, fascinator hats

- **Architecture + urban textures:** Roman columns, chain-link fences, graffitied concrete

- **Textiles:** Knots, knitting, crochet

- **Broad popular themes:** Nautical, fairy-tale, steampunk

- **Crafts:** Paper folding, decoupage, scrapbooking

- **Math and science:** Patterns, symbols, geometry

- **Printmaking:** Woodcut stamps, silk screen, lithography

- **Historical zeitgeists:** The 1920s, '50s, '80s

- **Folk art:** Tole-painted trays, handmade wallpaper, Easter eggs

- **Patterns:** Damask, houndstooth, tessellations

- **Jewelry:** Victorian lockets, tribal necklaces, jade carvings

- **Beautiful objects:** Instruments, antique furniture, mirror frames

- **Pop culture:** Movies, toys, games, music

- **Engineering and technology:** Circuit boards, gear mechanisms, simple machines

- **Spirituality:** Seven deadly sins, tarot, zodiac

- **Non-pie food:** Chocolate sculptures, fruit sculptures, sugar work

- **Round things:** Medallions, coins, manhole covers

Just search for "round art" on Pinterest and get ready to lose a couple of hours!

The final step is to create some way of capturing all your inspiration so that it's there when you need it. I'll leave it up to you to choose the method you like best—notebook, Pinterest boards, folder on your computer—just make sure you have a place to jot down your brilliant pie-deas as they come to you! I have notebooks filled with hundreds more Pie Art sketches than I will ever be able to create in one lifetime, but by constantly looking at the world around me with "pie eyes" and being open to inspiration, I am never short of ideas to fall back on when I need them!

PART 2

MAKING MEMORIES
(PROJECTS)

Are you ready to put your new skills to work and start creating some Pie Art magic? Heck yeah, you are!

I have striven to provide designs with broad cultural appeal, but what I would really love to see is for you to treat these high-level concepts as jumping-off points for your own creativity. To that end, I provide multiple Pie Modding options for each design, giving suggestions for alternate ways you can use the same techniques to create new Pie Art designs tailored to your and your family and friends' tastes. There is an assortment of beginner, intermediate, and advanced projects for you to choose from, with the beginner projects being suitable for twelve-year-old children, the advanced projects for people quite comfortable working with dough already, and the intermediate ones falling somewhere in between. But don't let those designations stop you from trying something that might look a little tricky!

Now, hey, ho, let's dough!

Lantern Festival Pie

The Lunar New Year and Spring Festival celebrations are huge occasions in my hometown of Vancouver. There are so many amazing public events, from the epic parade to the special lion and dragon dance performances, along with shadow puppet shows, martial arts demonstrations, amazing food vendors, gorgeous lantern displays, and red envelopes for everyone! My favorite of all the events is the Lantern Festival, and this pie, in red and gold, is in honor of this beautiful art form. I added the peach/cherry blossoms as a nod to another of my favorite local occasions that comes along shortly after—blossom-viewing season!

Level: Intermediate

Ingredients

+ Dough of your choice for 1 double-crust pie
+ Pasteurized egg whites (or almond milk if making a vegan pie)
+ Vanilla extract
+ Brown gel food color
+ Pink and green gel food colors (or colors of your choice)
+ Opaque white icing color
+ Gold, pearl, and pink luster dusts
+ Vodka (or any clear alcohol or extract to mix with the luster dusts)

Supplies

+ Parchment paper
+ Rolling pin
+ Paper templates
+ Food-safe precision blade
+ Assorted small flower- and leaf-shaped cutters (optional)
+ Ramekins or small containers to mix color and hold pasteurized egg whites
+ Pastry brush
+ Fondant sculpting tool (or toothpick)
+ Food-safe artist brushes
+ Toothpicks (for the gel food colors)
+ Baking sheet
+ Pie pan of your choice
+ Offset spatula

Dough of Your Choice

Select a dough that will retain small details, such as an all-lard or all-shortening shortcrust, a cookie-style dough, or a store-bought dough.

Base Pie

Create a base pie with a decorative crimped edge and any red-colored filling.

Resources

For instructions on downloading and printing the template for this pie, go to page 206. For edge-crimping suggestions, see page 60.

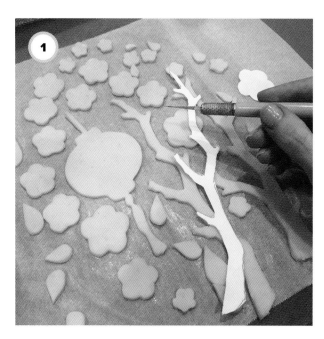

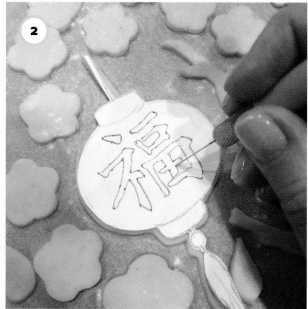

1. Roll out your dough ⅛ inch (3 mm) thick on a piece of parchment paper with your rolling pin. Place all the templates on the dough and cut out the shapes with your food-safe precision blade. Remove all the templates except the lantern template. (If you have flower- and leaf-shaped cutters on hand, you can use those in place of the flower and leaf templates.)

2. Poke guide holes through the lantern template with your precision blade to mark the lines of the Chinese characters.

3. Cut out the Chinese characters with your precision blade or score them with the fondant sculpting tool. (If cutting or scoring them is too tricky, simply paint the symbols now with brown gel food coloring mixed with some vanilla extract.)

4. Coat all the pieces in pasteurized egg whites with the pastry brush, then score bark lines and other details with the fondant sculpting tool.

5. Use a food-safe artist brush to give everything a vanilla wash with a mixture of vanilla extract and a tiny bit of brown gel food color, making sure the mixture seeps into the cracks. Now add color to your design with the gel food colors mixed with vanilla extract. (Add 1½ teaspoons of vanilla extract

to a ramekin, then dab a generous toothpick full of gel color on the edge of the ramekin. Dip your food-safe artist brush into the vanilla and then into the pigment on the side and paint away!) Paint the flowers pink, the leaves green, and the tree branches white. Carefully place the parchment paper with your decorative pieces onto a baking sheet and bake at 400°F (200°C; gas mark 6) for 10 minutes, or until golden brown.

6. While your decorative pieces are cooling, bake your base pie with a crimped edge. As soon as your base pie comes out of the oven, bubbling hot, carefully place the baked decorations on top with the offset spatula. Once everything is in place, add some gold and other touches of luster dusts mixed with a few drops of vodka to make it sparkle. Use the hashtags #LunarNewYearPie and #PiesAreAwesomeTheBook when you post pics of your version of this pie—I'd love to see what you create!

✶ Jessica's Tip ✶

Because the pieces will be sitting on a red background, you may want to give your tree bark a quick brushing with some opaque white icing color before or after baking to help it stand out.

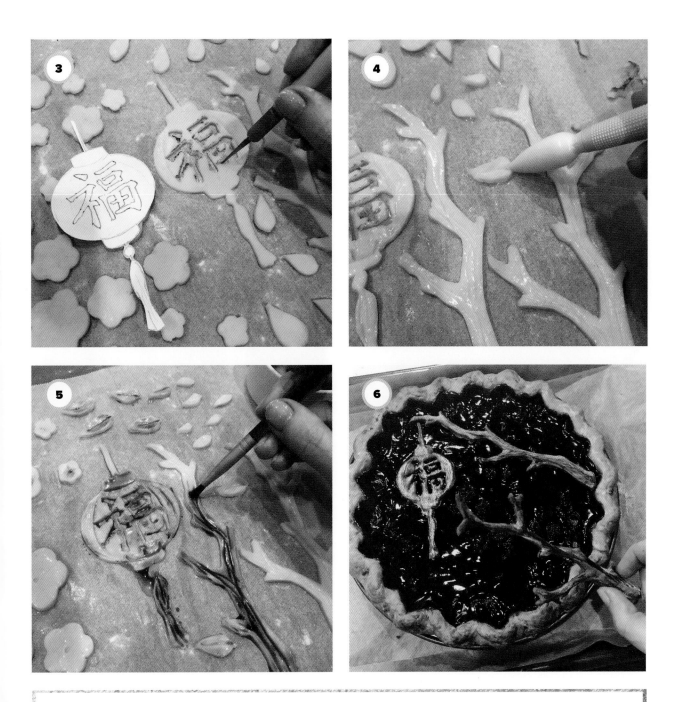

Pie-Modding Ideas

I think the "tree-with-blossoms" concept is lovely for any time of year. Consider trying it on different color fillings and with other decorations, such as fall leaves, birds, little hearts for Valentine's Day. There are many options!

Tic-Tac-Toe Pie

Food is an integral part of holiday celebrations—those times when we get to interact with the people who are important to us and have some fun. As such, the idea of "interactive food" has always fascinated me, including communal dishes like fondues, hot pots, chocolate fountains, and my latest invention: Pie Game Boards. I have created Scrabble pies, chess pies (not to be confused with chess-flavored pies!), checkers pies, and now this very simple tic-tac-toe game pie, with a fun Valentine's Day makeover. Win or lose, you still get to eat pie at the end of the date!

Level: Beginner

Ingredients

+ Dough of your choice for 1 double-crust pie
+ Whole egg wash
+ Pasteurized egg whites (or almond milk if making a vegan pie)
+ Clear sanding sugar

Supplies

+ Square pie or tart pan (or use a brownie pan)
+ Ramekins or small containers to hold egg wash and pasteurized egg whites
+ Pastry brush
+ Fork
+ Parchment paper
+ Stainless-steel ruler
+ Paper templates
+ Food-safe precision blade
+ Baking sheet
+ Cake lifter

✦ Jessica's Tip ✦

If you want to make the gaming surface even larger, consider making a "slab pie" directly on a baking sheet!

Dough of Your Choice
Good news! You can use any type of dough with this pie design.

Base Pie
Create a base pie with a decorative crimped edge and any red-colored filling in a square pan.

Resources
For instructions on downloading and printing the template for this pie, go to page 206. For edge-crimping suggestions, see page 60.

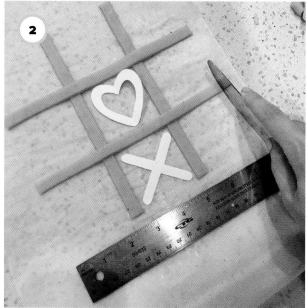

1. Roll out the dough for the base pie, and then line your square pie pan and create a crimped edge. Coat the bottom in egg wash with the pastry brush, dock (poke with a fork), and chill in the fridge for an hour before adding the filling. This will help prevent the bottom from becoming soggy in case you are using a slightly deeper-than-usual pie pan, such as a brownie pan.

2. Roll out some more dough ⅛ inch (3 mm) thick on a piece of parchment paper with your rolling pin. Cut four strips of dough, about ½ inch (1 cm) wide, the length of your pan, using the edge of the stainless-steel ruler. Coat the dough in pasteurized egg whites and place two of the strips perpendicular to the other two to create a nine-square grid. Size your "game-piece" templates to fit within these squares.

3. Cut your game pieces out of the dough with your food-safe precision blade. Give them a coating of pasteurized egg whites, then sprinkle them with the clear sanding sugar. Feel free to make extra pieces! This type of game piece has a tendency to go missing . . .

4. Carefully place the parchment paper with your grid and game pieces onto a baking sheet and bake at 400°F (200°C; gas mark 6) for 8 to 10 minutes, or until golden brown.

5. While the grid and game pieces cool, bake your base pie. As soon as your base pie comes out of the oven, bubbling hot, carefully place the grid on top with the cake lifter.

6. Now set out your pie game board and game pieces and challenge your sweetheart to a round. Winner gets the first slice! Use the hashtags #TicTacToePie and #PiesAreAwesomeTheBook when you post pics of your version of this pie—I'd love to see what you create!

Pie-Modding Ideas

What other simple games do you think you could play on the surface of a pie? How about backgammon, mancala, or go. Or if you are feeling really ambitious, Chutes and Ladders!

Pi Pie

What began as a holiday for math nerds has quickly taken over the baking world, as pro and amateur pie-oneers alike use it as an opportunity to celebrate the world's favorite pastry. Pi Day potluck (or pie-luck) parties are now standard practice on this most awesome of days, March 14 (aka 3.14), and won't you be the popular geek if you show up and throw down this crusty creation!

Level: Beginner

Ingredients

+ Dough of your choice for 1 double-crust pie
+ Pasteurized egg whites (or almond milk if making a vegan pie)
+ Whole egg wash

Supplies

+ Parchment paper
+ Rolling pin
+ Pie pan of your choice
+ Food-safe precision blade
+ Paper templates
+ 1- to 2-inch (2.5 to 5 cm) round cookie cutter
+ Stainless-steel ruler
+ Ramekins or small containers to hold pasteurized egg whites and egg wash
+ Pastry brush
+ Fondant sculpting tool (or toothpick)
+ Assorted small flower-shaped plunger cutters (optional)
+ Baking sheet
+ Cake lifter

Dough of Your Choice

You may want to steer clear of all-butter doughs for this pie. Other than that, anything goes!

Base Pie

Create an infinity-edge base pie with the filling extending all the way to the edges (see page 60). Any flavor will do!

Resources

For instructions on downloading and printing the template for this pie, go to page 206.

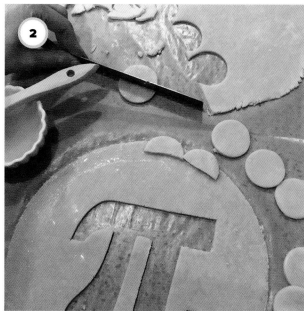

1. Roll out your dough ⅛ inch (3 mm) thick on a piece of parchment paper with your rolling pin. Lay your pie pan facedown on the rolled-out dough and cut out a circle the size of your pie pan with your food-safe precision blade. Then place the pi symbol template in the center of the cutout dough circle and cut out the shape.

2. Using the round cookie cutter and the stainless-steel ruler to cut them in half, cut out enough semicircles from the dough scraps to go all the way around the perimeter of your dough circle. Coat your dough in pasteurized egg whites with the pastry brush and paste the semicircles down around the perimeter.

3. Use your fondant sculpting tool to score a line from the center of the semicircles down to the dough circle. This not only adds a decorative touch, but also helps adhere the two layers together.

4. Using the templates, cut out as many flower shapes from the dough as will fit inside the pi symbol. (If you have flower-shaped plunger cutters on hand, you can use those in place of the templates. If you don't have any small cutters and don't want to cut out the flowers,

you can roll different-sizes balls of dough and flatten them into little disks to create a polka-dot design instead!)

5. Give everything a generous coating of egg wash with the pastry brush. Carefully place the parchment paper with your top decoration onto a baking sheet and bake at 400°F (200°C; gas mark 6) for 10 to 14 minutes, or until golden brown.

> ★ **Jessica's Tip** ★
>
> Take a photo of your flower placement while it is on the baking sheet so that it will be easier to put the flowers in their correct spots on the pie later if any get loose!

6. While your top decoration cools, bake your base pie with an infinity edge. As soon as your base pie comes out of the oven, bubbling hot, carefully place the top decoration on top with the cake lifter. Place any free-floating flowers inside the pi symbol by hand. Use the hashtags #PiDayPie and #PiesAreAwesomeTheBook when you post pics of your version of this pie—I'd love to see what you create!

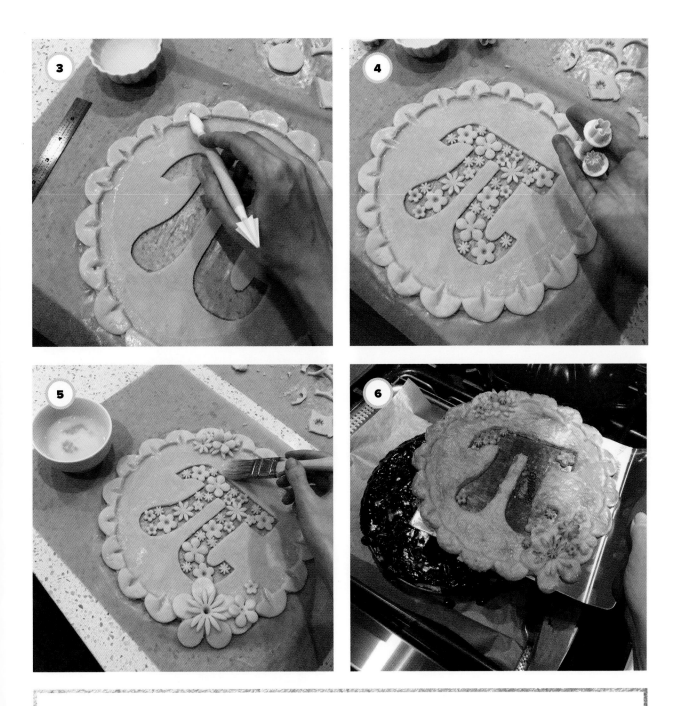

Pie-Modding Ideas

While I am a big fan of the pi symbol (it just happens to be in my logo!), why not branch out into other symbols and fill those with little cutout shapes? Maybe your friend's initial or a treble clef for the music lover in your life?

Leprechaun Hat Pie

Top o' the mornin' and tip o' the hat to ya! I'm one-quarter Irish, so of course I must make a big deal out of St. Patrick's Day every year . . . even if actual Irish people don't. Ha! But it is a ton of fun to make green treats with my son, hide gold coins, and wear green so that the leprechauns don't pinch us! This pie fits right in with the rest of our sparkly festivities, and I hope your family will love it too.

Level: Intermediate

Ingredients

+ Dough of your choice for 1 double-crust pie
+ Pasteurized egg whites (or almond milk if making a vegan pie)
+ Vanilla extract
+ Brown gel food color
+ Black gel food color
+ Gold and green luster dusts
+ Vodka (or any clear alcohol or extract to mix with the luster dusts)
+ Green sanding sugar and nonpareils
+ Green sugar pearls or dragées

Supplies

+ Parchment paper
+ Rolling pin
+ Pie pan of your choice
+ Pastry crimper/wheel (optional)
+ Stainless-steel ruler
+ Paper templates
+ Food-safe precision blade
+ Ramekins or small containers to hold pasteurized egg whites and mix color
+ Pastry brush
+ Fondant sculpting tool (or toothpick)
+ Food-safe artist brushes
+ Toothpick (for the gel food colors)
+ Baking sheet
+ Cake lifter

Dough of Your Choice

The hat and shamrock shapes are simple enough that you should be able to get away with using any type of pie dough with the possible exception of puff pastry.

Base Pie

Create an infinity-edge base pie with the filling extending all the way to the edges (see page 60). I dyed this apple filling with gel food color, so any filling that is light enough to take color will do.

Resources

For instructions on downloading and printing the template for this pie, go to page 206.

1. Roll out your dough ⅛ inch (3 mm) thick on a piece of parchment paper with your rolling pin. Lay your pie pan facedown on the rolled-out dough and cut out a circle the size of your pie pan with the pastry crimper (if you don't have one, you can just use your food-safe precision blade).

2. With the stainless-steel ruler, very lightly score some decorative background lines into your dough circle, alternating thick and thin strips. Be careful not to score the dough too deep or it may separate in the oven! These are just guides for painting the stripes later.

3. Place the hat templates on the center of the dough and cut out the shapes with your food-safe precision blade.

4. Coat the dough with pasteurized egg whites using the pastry brush.

5. Cut out the hat band and buckle templates from scrap pieces of dough and place them on the design using the pasteurized egg whites as glue.

6. From your scrap dough, cut out an assortment of the large and small shamrock templates. Coat them in pasteurized egg whites, then score lines in them with the fondant sculpting tool.

(continued on page 97)

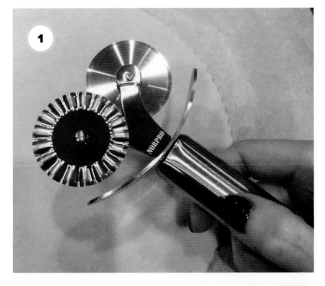

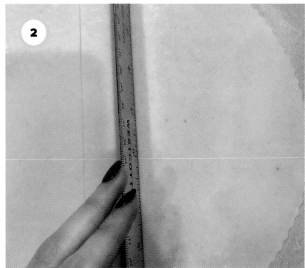

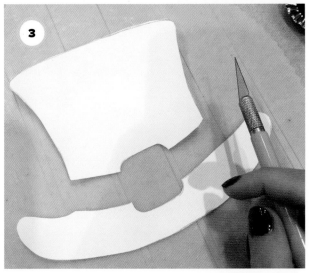

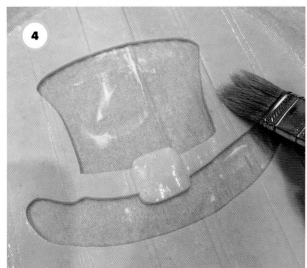

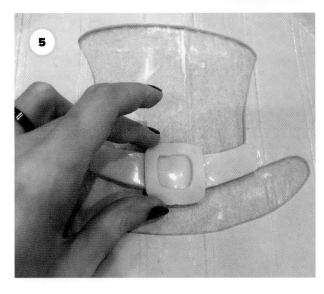

LEPRECHAUN HAT PIE

95

(continued from page 94)

7. Use a food-safe artist brush to give the hat band and buckle, shamrock shapes, and alternating background stripes a vanilla wash with a mixture of vanilla extract and a tiny bit of brown gel food color, making sure the mixture seeps into the cracks.

8. Paint the thick background lines covered in vanilla wash black with the black gel food color mixed with vanilla extract, but leave the thin lines brown. (Add 1½ teaspoons of vanilla extract to a ramekin, then dab a generous toothpick full of gel color on the edge of the ramekin. Dip your food-safe artist brush into the vanilla and then into the pigment on the side and paint away!) The thin lines will be tinted gold with luster dust postbake, and the gold will pop best if the underlying color remains brown.

9. Place the shamrock shapes around the pie top wherever you think they look good.

10. Using the fondant sculpting tool, make ten or twelve divots any place you like that will house the green sugar pearls postbake. This will help keep them from rolling around all over the place when you move the pie! Carefully place the parchment paper with your top decoration onto

a baking sheet and bake at 400°F (200°C; gas mark 6) for 12 minutes, or until golden brown.

11. While your top decoration cools, bake your base pie with an infinity edge. As soon as your base pie comes out of the oven, bubbling hot, use the cake lifter to place the top decoration on top. Lightly press down for 10 seconds so that the top and base fuse together. With your gold and green luster dusts mixed with a few drops of vodka, paint the thin background stripes and hat buckle gold and the shamrocks green.

12. Sprinkle the green sanding sugar and small pearl sprinkles on the exposed filling of the pie and place the green sugar pearls in the divots you made in step 10. Use the hashtags #StPatricksDayPie and #PiesAreAwesomeTheBook when you post pics of your version of this pie—I'd love to see what you create!

✦ Jessica's Tip ✦

If your sugar pearls keep popping out of the divots and rolling around, you can dip them in a little bit of the filling to help them stick in place.

Pie-Modding Ideas

I find the black-and-gold background stripes to be really striking and think they would make a great backdrop for all sorts of special-occasion pies. Try cutting out a Christmas tree shape and adding multicolor sprinkle "ornaments," or maybe a teacup or teapot shape with dough flowers inside for a classy tea party offering!

Bunny Pie

Who's ready to hop into Easter baking? "Pie" may not be the first thing we think of when we think of Easter treats, but after the kids peep this delicious offering in the center of the table, you may just have a new tradition on your hands!

Level: Intermediate

Ingredients

+ Dough of your choice for 1½ double-crust pies
+ Pasteurized egg whites (or almond milk if making a vegan pie)
+ Vanilla extract
+ Brown gel food color
+ Opaque white icing color
+ Pink, green, and teal gel food colors (or colors of your choice)
+ Edible adhesive (such as leftover filling or sugar glue)
+ Pink, green, and gold luster dusts (optional)
+ Vodka (or any clear alcohol or extract to mix with the luster dusts) (optional)
+ Pink sanding sugar

Supplies

+ Parchment paper
+ Rolling pin
+ Paper templates
+ Food-safe precision blade
+ Assorted small flower- and nature-shaped plunger cutters (optional)
+ Ramekins or small containers to hold pasteurized egg whites and mix color
+ Pastry brush
+ Fondant sculpting tool (or toothpick)
+ Food-safe artist brushes
+ Toothpicks (for the gel food colors)
+ Pie pan of your choice
+ Baking sheet
+ Cake lifter

Dough of Your Choice

Select a relatively non-puffy dough for this more detailed pie, such as cookie-style, shortening-based, or store-bought.

Base Pie

Create a base pie with a decorative crimped edge. Because you are adding sanding sugar to the top of this pie, you may want to opt for a tart filling, such as cranberry or Granny Smith apple, or forgo adding sweetener to the filling altogether and simply use fruit and thickener.

Resources

For instructions on downloading and printing the template for this pie, go to page 206. For edge-crimping suggestions, see page 60.

1. Roll out your dough ⅛ inch (3 mm) thick on a piece of parchment paper with your rolling pin. Place your paper templates on the rolled-out dough and cut out all the shapes with your food-safe precision blade. Remove the templates. (If you have flower- and nature-shaped plunger cutters on hand, you can use those in place of the flower templates.)

2. Coat the scalloped-edge medallion in pasteurized egg whites with the pastry brush.

3. Place the "ground" piece on the medallion, give it a coat of pasteurized egg whites, and then, using your fingernails, "squinch" up little bits of the dough to create the illusion of a mossy forest floor.

4. Coat all the pieces in pasteurized egg whites, then paste the bunny, the smaller butterfly that sits on the bunny's nose, and some flowers on the medallion.

5. With the fondant sculpting tool, score detail lines in the bunny. Score a line to demarcate the tummy, a curved line for the mouth, a smaller curved line for the closed eye, two curved lines inside the ear, and some "scruffy fur marks" around the leg, tail, and back of his neck.

6. Once you are happy with the details, use a food-safe artist brush to give everything a vanilla wash with a mixture of vanilla extract and a tiny bit of brown gel food color, making sure the mixture seeps into the cracks.

(continued on page 103)

(continued from page 100)

7. Paint the dough around the perimeter of the bunny with brown gel food color. Drip some plain vanilla extract just outside of the brown outline you just painted, and with your food-safe artist brush, blot the brown color into the plain vanilla to create a gradient fade. This will help the central figure really pop after it bakes!

8. Paint the bunny figure with the white icing color, keeping just shy of the edges so that the white does not bleed into the scored lines where the vanilla wash is.

9. Paint the grass, flowers, and butterflies with the gel food colors mixed with vanilla extract. (Add 1½ teaspoons of vanilla extract to a ramekin, then dab a generous toothpick full of gel color on the edge of the ramekin. Dip your food-safe artist brush into the vanilla and then into the pigment on the side and paint away!) Add a little pink cheek to finish your bunny.

10. If desired, add a few dots of white icing color to the butterflies to amp up the details of their wings. When you are happy with your composition, carefully place the parchment paper with your top decorations onto a baking sheet and bake at 400°F (200°C; gas mark 6) for 10 to 14 minutes, or until golden brown.

11. While your top decorations cool, bake your base pie with a crimped edge. As soon as your base pie comes out of the oven, bubbling hot, carefully place the top decorations on top with the cake lifter. Using a dot of the filling or sugar glue as edible adhesive, add the larger butterfly and additional flowers to the pie. Now if you like, you can add a few pops of the luster dusts mixed with a few drops of vodka to the flowers and butterflies.

12. Sprinkle the pink sanding sugar on the exposed filling just before you are ready to serve the pie. Use the hashtags #BunnyPie and #PiesAreAwesomeTheBook when you post pics of your version of this pie—I'd love to see what you create!

Pie-Modding Ideas

If you have a favorite cartoon character that is comprised of relatively simple shapes, you can trace a template for them off your computer screen and create your own custom composition in the same way you just made this bunny! Almost any simple character will look great in the center of a pastry medallion like this.

Folk Art Bee Pie

Many Earth Day celebrations feature treats in the shape of the planet or maybe a tree, but I felt like bees deserved their own tribute, given how important they are to us. Indeed, they are widely considered to be the most important beings on Earth! Whether we realize it or not, bees are vital to nature, and as pollinators a critical part of our ecosystem, which is sadly facing threats from many sides currently. But there are things we can do at home to help give them a fighting chance, including planting bee-friendly plants and spreading the awareness of their plight with delicious pies!

Level: Intermediate

Ingredients

+ Dough of your choice for 1½ double-crust pies
+ Pasteurized egg whites (or almond milk if making a vegan pie)
+ Brown and green gel food colors (or colors of your choice)
+ Vanilla extract
+ Gold and green luster dusts
+ Vodka (or any clear alcohol or extract to mix with the luster dusts)
+ Gold sugar pearls or dragées

Supplies

+ Parchment paper
+ Rolling pin
+ Paper templates
+ Food-safe precision blade
+ Assorted small leaf- and flower-shaped plunger cutters (optional)
+ Ramekins or small containers to hold pasteurized egg whites and mix color
+ Pastry brush
+ Fondant sculpting tool (or toothpick)
+ Food-safe artist brushes
+ Toothpicks (for the gel food colors)
+ Baking sheet
+ Pie pan of your choice
+ Metal spatula

Dough of Your Choice

Any dough with the exception of an all-butter pastry should work for this pie, but if you really want your details to be crisp, consider using a cookie-style dough for the top crust. You can always use a butter-based dough for the crust of the base pie.

Base Pie

Create a base pie with a decorative crimped edge. I used my Banana Cream Cheese Icebox Pie Filling on page 225 but flavored it with honey instead of banana.

Resources

For instructions on downloading and printing the template for this pie, go to page 206. For edge-crimping suggestions, see page 60.

✦ Jessica's Tip ✦

If you don't want to make a cream pie, you can still achieve the high-contrast look by using a dark filling, like blueberry or blackberry, and keeping the dough pieces unpainted. It will have a lovely folk art effect—and save you some time!

1. Roll out your dough ⅛ inch (3 mm) thick on a piece of parchment paper with your rolling pin. Place all the templates on the rolled-out dough and cut out the shapes with your food-safe precision blade. (If you have leaf- and flower-shaped cutters on hand, you can use those in place of the templates. Your composition will look a little different than mine, but ain't nothing wrong with that!)

2. Generously coat all the dough pieces in pasteurized egg whites with the pastry brush.

3. Using the fondant sculpting tool, score lines in your pieces to add details (refer to the photo for step 9 on page 108). To make the stripes on the bee's butt look a little more realistic, make horizontal strokes in a curved arc. See the next four steps for scoring lines in the bee wings.

4.–8. Reference the photos to see how to score the lines in the wings.

(*continued on page 109*)

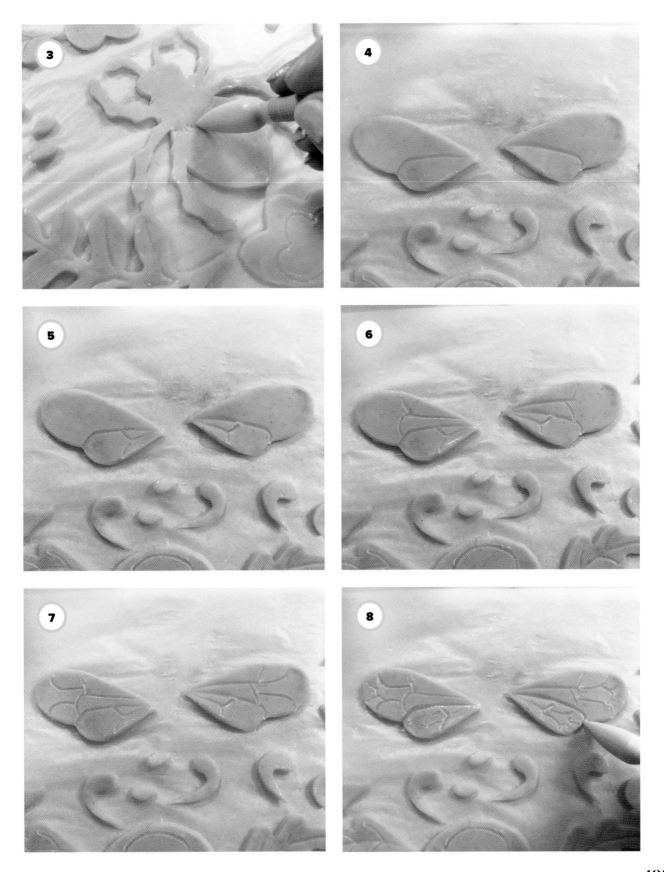

(continued from page 106)

9. Place the wings on top of the bee's body

10. Now you can paint your pieces with the gel food colors mixed with vanilla extract. (Add 1½ teaspoons of vanilla extract to a ramekin, then dab a generous toothpick full of gel color on the edge of the ramekin. Dip your food-safe artist brush into the vanilla and then into the pigment on the side and paint away!) I painted the bee dark brown, leaving alternate stripes unpainted (they will be painted gold postbake), and the leaves two different tones of green. But you should choose colors that will contrast the most with your base pie background. When you are satisfied with your paint job, carefully place the parchment paper with your bee and decorative pieces onto the baking sheet and bake at 400°F (200°C; gas mark 6) for 8 to 12 minutes, or until golden brown.

11. Let your pieces cool, then use the gold and green luster dusts mixed with a few drops of vodka to highlight a few details here and there, such as the bee's stripes.

12. While the pieces are cooling, bake your base pie. If using a filling similar to mine, you will need to blind-bake the shell before adding the filling (see page 226 and the Resources section on page 228

Pie-Modding Ideas

Are bees not your bag? Look up "circle folk art" on Pinterest, and you'll be overloaded with inspiring compositions to help you create your own signature folk art–style pies!

for instructions on how to blind-bake pie shells). Make the pie filling, pipe or spoon it into the cooled blind-baked shell, and let the base pie set in the refrigerator for 2 hours. When your base pie is set, carefully place the bee in the center of the pie with the metal spatula.

13. Begin placing the rest of the baked pieces, starting from the center and working outward. (If using a base pie with a baked filling, place the bee and decorative pieces on the base pie when it comes out of the oven, bubbling hot.)

14. As a final touch, add some gold sugar pearls to nicely offset the gold luster-dust details. Use the hashtags #EarthDayPie and #PiesAreAwesomeTheBook when you post pics of your version of this pie—I'd love to come see what you create!

Quilt Pie

Okay, maybe not every mother is into quilting (mine isn't), but somebody's mother out there somewhere has to be, right? I love this pie design as well as the technique used here in general, because you can basically make it with your eyes closed—the stencils do all the work for you! But don't tell your Mum that. Best Mother's Day present ever!

Level: Beginner

Ingredients

+ Dough of your choice for 1 double-crust pie
+ Pasteurized egg whites (or almond milk if making a vegan pie)
+ Ground cinnamon
+ Whole egg wash

Supplies

+ 4 acetate stencils, each with a different pattern (or food-safe found objects to use as stencils)
+ Parchment paper
+ Rolling pin
+ Pie pan of your choice
+ Food-safe precision blade
+ Stainless-steel ruler
+ Ramekins or small containers to hold pasteurized egg whites and egg wash
+ Pastry brush
+ Fork
+ Fondant sculpting tool (or toothpick)
+ Baking sheet
+ Metal spatula or cake lifter

Dough of Your Choice
Good news! Any dough will do for this pie design.

Base Pie
This project and the Harvest Tree Pie on page 154 are the only two projects in the book in which the top and bottom of the pie are combined and baked together with a decorative crimped edge. This means you can pile your filling as high as you like! Consider taking this opportunity to experiment with mile-high apple pie filling.

Resources
For edge-crimping suggestions, see page 60.

1. If your stencils are new, wash them by hand in soapy water and pat dry with paper towels. If you don't have stencils, you can make your own with hole punches, ribbons, bits of lace, or anything with an interesting pattern or shape!

2. Roll out your dough ⅛ inch (3 mm) thick on a piece of parchment paper with your rolling pin. Lay your pie pan facedown on the rolled-out dough and cut out a circle the size of your pie pan with your food-safe precision blade.

3. Cut the circle into four equal sections using the stainless-steel ruler. Freeze the dough solid as is, and then separate the quadrants from each other on the parchment. Don't try to move the quadrants if they aren't cold enough! The dough will distort, and your pie will get a little more rustic looking than you may want.

4. Coat each quadrant in pasteurized egg whites with the pastry brush.

5. Place a different stencil on top of each quadrant and sprinkle the ground cinnamon on top.

★ Jessica's Tip ★

Place the two quadrants that are going to be the darkest in color and the two quadrants that are going to be the lightest diagonally across from each other to create the most balanced composition.

6. Tap the cinnamon into the dough with your fingers to ensure good adhesion, making sure the exposed parts of each stencil are well covered. Carefully brush the excess powder off the stencils.

(continued on page 115)

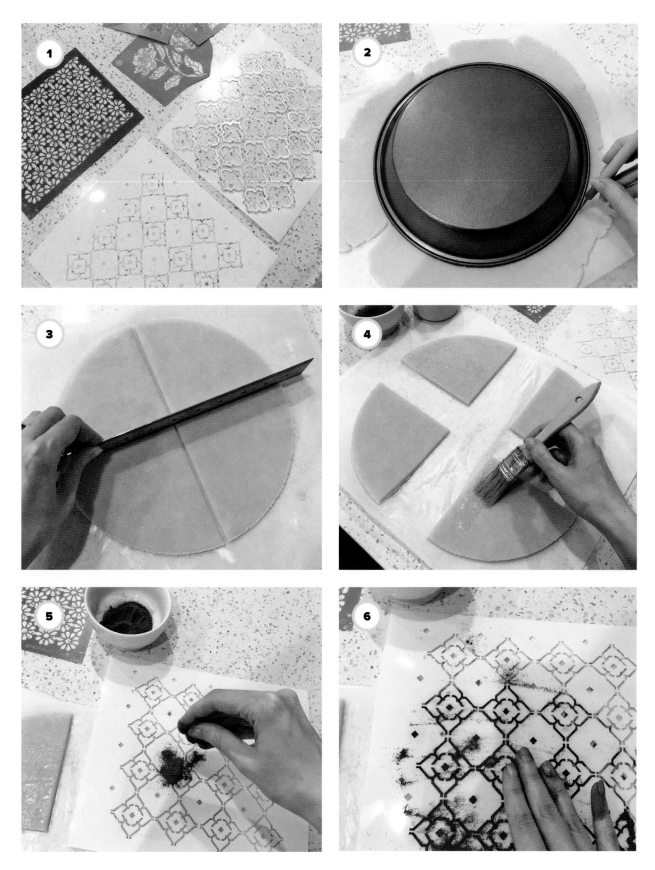

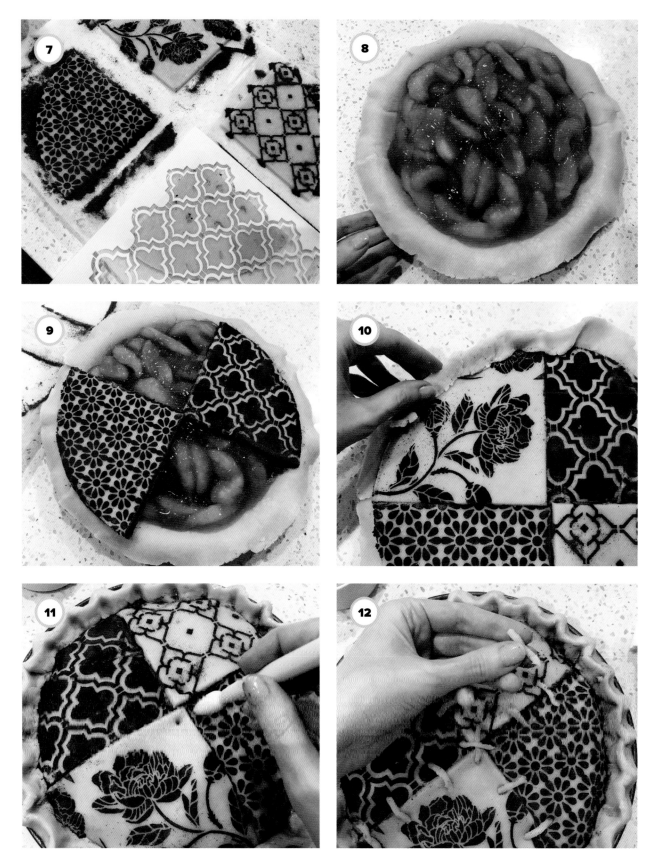

(continued from page 112)

7. After you have removed all the loose powder, lift each stencil straight up and away from the dough. You can just pop them in the sink to handwash later.

8. Place your stenciled quadrants back in the freezer while you prepare your base pie. Now prepare your base pie as you would for a crimped-edge pie—roll out a sheet of dough 3 inches (7.5 cm) larger than your pie pan all around, transfer it to the pan, coat the bottom with egg wash, dock (poke) the dough with a fork, and add the filling. Wrap a golf ball–size ball of leftover dough in plastic wrap in the fridge. You will use this later to create the "stitches" for your quilt.

9. Once your base pie is ready to bake, carefully place the frozen stenciled quadrants on top with the metal spatula.

10. Fold over the overhanging dough, tuck in the quadrants, and crimp the edges.

11. With the fondant sculpting tool, poke little stitch holes along the edges of the quadrants.

★ Jessica's Tip ★

If you are feeling fancy and ambitious, you can bake some extra dough sunflowers and add them on top of the pie postbake to make your Mum's day that much sunnier!

12. Remove your ball of spare dough from the fridge and cut some tiny strips of dough to be the "stitches." Dip the ends of the dough stitches in pasteurized egg whites and paste them in place so that they look like they are connecting the holes. Cover the edges of your pie with foil and bake on a baking sheet at 400°F (200°C; gas mark 6) for 40 minutes. Remove the foil and add some egg wash to the crimped edges, then bake for another 20 minutes, or until the filling has been bubbling for 5 minutes. Use the hashtags #MothersDayPie and #PiesAreAwesomeTheBook when you post pics of your version of this pie—I'd love to see what you create!

Pie-Modding Ideas

Try different colors of edible powder! You could use activated charcoal, matcha powder, paprika, or dehydrated dragon fruit powder to name a few. You may also try stamping the pattern on the dough quadrants with a sponge brush and more traditional food paints. This will allow you to achieve cool effects, like rainbow or color gradients.

Shirt and Tie Pie

Is your dad tired of getting the same tie for Father's Day every year? Why not mix it up a little this year with a "tie pie" instead! I promise this gift won't sit in the back of his sock drawer for ten years, and even better, it's a gift the whole family can enjoy at your Father's Day celebration! (Plus, it will only cost you about five bucks . . . but don't tell him that!)

Level: Beginner

Ingredients

+ Dough of your choice for 1 double-crust pie, plus a little extra for the pocket
+ Pasteurized egg whites (or almond milk if making a vegan pie)
+ Brown gel food color
+ Vanilla extract
+ Opaque white icing color
+ Chocolate-flavored rice balls or other edible decorations

Supplies

+ Parchment paper
+ Rolling pin
+ Pie pan of your choice
+ Stainless-steel ruler
+ Paper templates
+ Food-safe precision blade
+ Fondant sculpting tool (or toothpick)
+ Ramekins or small containers to hold pasteurized egg whites and mix color
+ Pastry brush
+ Food-safe artist brushes
+ Baking sheet
+ Cake lifter

Dough of Your Choice

With the exception of puff pastry, any dough will work with this design. I used an all-butter dough.

Base Pie

What filling should you choose? Why dad's favorite, of course! Create an infinity-edge base pie with the filling extending all the way to the edges (see page 60).

Resources

For instructions on downloading and printing the template for this pie, go to page 206.

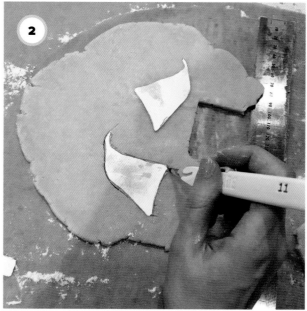

1. Roll out your pie dough ⅛ inch (3 mm) thick on a piece of parchment paper with your rolling pin. Lay your pie pan facedown on the rolled-out dough and cut out a circle the size of your pie pan with your food-safe precision blade. With the stainless-steel ruler, very lightly score some evenly spaced vertical lines. I scored twelve lines.

2. On a separate piece of dough, place your templates for the shirt collar, pocket, and button and cut out the shapes. Remove the templates.

3. Coat the dough circle and cutout pieces in pasteurized egg whites with the pastry brush, then paste the shirt collar and pocket onto the dough circle. Using the fondant sculpting tool, score the details on the pocket's button.

4. Position the tie template on the dough circle and cut out the shape.

5. Paint the stripes, button, and inside of the collar with brown gel food mixed with a few drops of vanilla extract and the collar and pocket with the white icing color. Carefully place the parchment paper with your top decorations onto a baking sheet and bake at 400°F (200°C; gas mark 6) for 10 to 14 minutes, or until golden brown.

✦ Jessica's Tip ✦

If your dad's favorite pie filling just happens to be the same color as pie dough, consider painting the entire shirt brown, white, or some other color so that there will be enough contrast between the tie and the background.

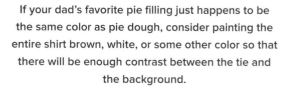

6. While your top decoration is cooling, bake your base pie with an infinity edge. As soon as your base pie comes out of the oven, bubbling hot, carefully place the top decoration on top with the cake lifter. Lightly press down for 10 seconds so that the top and base fuse together. Finish off your tie with the chocolate-flavored rice balls or whatever edible bling you think your dad will love best. Use the hashtags #TiePie and #PiesAreAwesomeTheBook when you post pics of your version of this pie. I'd love to see what you create!

Pie-Modding Ideas

Is your dad more of a sweater guy than a shirt and tie guy? Mix it up by adding a sweater collar instead of a dress-shirt collar and use mini cutters to create a repeating pattern on the sweater. You can kick things up a notch by scoring in tiny sweater stitches too!

Stars and Stripes Pie

Can't decide whether to serve the guests at your Independence Day cookout a cherry pie or a blueberry pie this year? Why not both! This divided-filling pie offers the best of both worlds while giving a festive nod to both the flag and the fireworks displays. Though the fireworks are guaranteed to pack a big bang, they'll have nothing on the impact this awesome pie will make on your friends and family!

Level: Intermediate

Ingredients

+ Dough of your choice for 1½ double-crust pies
+ Pasteurized egg whites (or almond milk if making a vegan pie)
+ Whipped topping

Supplies

+ Parchment paper
+ Rolling pin
+ Paper templates
+ Food-safe precision blade
+ Star-shaped cutters (optional)
+ Baking sheet
+ Pie pan of your choice
+ Ramekin or small container to hold pasteurized egg whites
+ Pastry brush
+ Small spoon
+ Metal spatula

Dough of Your Choice

For this pie you can use cookie-style, all-butter, all-shortening, all-lard, or vegan dough interchangeably.

Base Pie

Create a base pie with a decorative crimped edge and two types of filling: cherry and blueberry.

 Jessica's Tip

If your guests don't like the idea of two types of filling together, you can always make the whole thing an apple pie by just dividing the filling between two bowls and mixing in a little blue and red food coloring!

Resources

For instructions on downloading and printing the template for this pie, go to page 206. For edge-crimping suggestions, see page 60.

1. Roll out a full sheet of dough ⅛ inch (3 mm) thick on a piece of parchment paper with your rolling pin. Place the star and stripe (ray) templates on the rolled-out dough and cut out the shapes with your food-safe precision blade. I cut out nineteen stars of varying sizes and nine rays, though I only used six—it's always good to have some extras! Remove the templates. (If you have star-shaped cutters on hand, you can use them in place of the template.) Don't move the stars once you've cut them—they are finicky. Cut them in place on parchment paper so that you don't risk making them misshapen. Bake the stars and rays at 400°F (200°C; gas mark 6) for 10 to 12 minutes, or until golden brown. Set aside to cool.

2. Line your pie pan with the dough of your choice and create a crimped edge. Poke a small guide dot in the center of your base pie shell. Line up the template for the dividers from the center of this dot outward and lightly score along one side of the template. Lift and reposition the template and score along the same side until you have scored eight curved lines, equally spaced around the bottom of your pie.

3. Roll out the remaining dough ⅛ inch (3 mm) thick and cut out the six divider panel shapes. Give both the base pie and the dividers a generous coating of pasteurized egg whites with the pastry brush.

4. Put your fillings in bowls and have small spoons handy. Place your divider panels and smooth the edges and bottoms into the sides and bottom of the pie shell with the back of your fingernail.

5. With a small spoon, add the cherry filling to the four smaller panels opposite one other. Don't worry if the divider walls shift around on you

a little at this stage; you will be able to fix this once all the filling is in.

6. Now spoon the blueberry filling into the remaining two panels. If your dividers have shifted at all, add a little bit of extra filling, or scoop out a bit to nudge them back into place. Bake your base pie at 400°F (200°C; gas mark 6) for about an hour, or until the filling has been bubbling for at least 5 minutes. If your filling is not precooked, you may want to cover the crust edges in foil for the first 45 minutes so that they don't cook faster than the filling.

7. As soon as your base pies come out of the oven, bubbling hot, carefully use the metal spatula to place the rays on top of the dividers and the stars on top of the blueberry sections.

8. When the pie has completely cooled, and just before you are about to serve it, pipe or spoon the whipped topping over two of the cherry sections opposite each other. Use the hashtags #StarsAndStripesPie and #PiesAreAwesomeTheBook when you post pics of your version of this pie—I'd love to see what you create!

✦ Jessica's Tip ✦

If you are finding that your divider dough panels are not baked through, next time make them a bit thinner, paint some jam on each side as a moisture barrier, and then freeze the base pie shell for an hour before adding the filling. Or, if you want to get really fancy, you can par-bake your shell for 15 minutes at 400°F (200°C; gas mark 6) first. Just make sure you add some sort of pie weight you can easily remove after baking so that your carefully placed divider walls don't sink in.

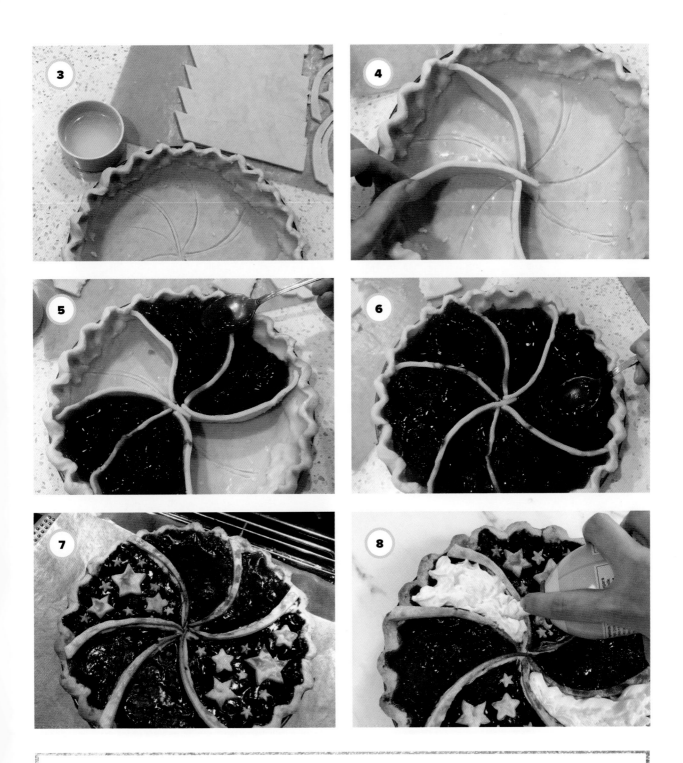

Pie-Modding Ideas

This style of pie can be a festive treat for just about any holiday by simply swapping out the colors of filling and the decorative cutouts you place on top. You can alternate cherry and apple fillings to create a peppermint-swirl design for Christmas or make a rainbow for Pride!

Paris Skyline Pie

Little known fact about me: I am both a Canadian and a French citizen, so I thought it would be fun to throw a little Bastille Day action into our holiday mix. July 14 is the Fête nationale in France, in which, similar to Canada Day and the Fourth of July, folks celebrate with parties, fireworks, and, of course, awesome food, like this Paris Skyline Pie! For this design, I chose a few of my favorite Parisian landmarks and created simplified silhouettes of them. By stacking layers of dough to create the foreground, mid-ground, and background, I have created an illusion of depth that only needs a bit of highlighting with some vanilla wash to complete the effect. Since the City of Lights shines brightest at night, I chose a dark blueberry filling to act as the night sky, sprinkling it liberally with golden stars.

Level: Advanced

Ingredients

+ Dough of your choice to make 1½ double-crust pies
+ Pasteurized egg whites (or almond milk if making a vegan pie)
+ Vanilla extract
+ Brown gel food color
+ Gold star sprinkles

Supplies

+ Parchment paper
+ Rolling pin
+ Paper templates
+ Food-safe precision blade
+ Pencil
+ Pie pan of your choice
+ Ramekins or small containers to hold pasteurized egg whites and mix vanilla wash
+ Pastry brush
+ Fondant sculpting tool (or toothpick)
+ Small flower-shaped plunger cutters (optional)
+ Food-safe artist brush
+ Baking sheet

Dough of Your Choice
Lard, shortening, or butter-based doughs will all work well with this design, but steer clear of puff pastry, or you'll risk losing all your carefully sculpted details!

Base Pie
Create an infinity-edge base pie with the filling extending all the way to the edges (see page 60). Select any dark filling for a "night sky." I've chosen a blueberry filling for this pie, but you could use blackberry, mincemeat, or just coat the top of any filling with dark-colored sanding sugar.

Resources
For instructions on downloading and printing the template for this pie, go to page 206.

1. Roll out your dough ⅛ inch (3 mm) thick on a piece of parchment paper with your rolling pin. Place your templates on the rolled-out dough and cut out all the shapes with your food-safe precision blade. You may need two pieces of parchment to fit all of them.

2. Coat all the pieces in pasteurized egg whites with the pastry brush. It's time to start layering them! If your dough is at all sticky or hard to lift without cracking, just pop your parchment sheet in the freezer for a couple minutes, then use a spatula to lift up the pieces. Any cracks can be easily patched and smoothed out with pasteurized egg whites. Lay your pie pan facedown on a piece of parchment paper and trace around it with a pencil so that you can layer your dough pieces within the circle as a guide. Start with the buildings as the base layer, then top the buildings with the bridge, followed by the banner on the bridge. Place the trees and moon, and then, finally, the shrubs as the top layer in the foreground.

3. Now for the fun part! Add the details. Because our buildings are so tiny, we won't be able to sculpt any details to add to them, but we can still create the illusion of depth by pushing back certain areas with the fondant sculpting tool. Just make sure the dough is well coated in pasteurized egg whites before you do this so that it doesn't crack.

4. Working from left to right, score the lines in Notre-Dame, the Moulin Rouge, the Eiffel Tower, the Arc de Triomphe, and Sacré-Cœur.

5. I've simplified the shapes quite a bit, so feel free carve the same details into your buildings. But if you are feeling ambitious, you can look up the photos for each of these monuments and add some extra detail!

6. If you're having any trouble carving the details, check out the section Sculpting Pie Dough on page 50 for some tips and tricks before you move on to finishing your skyline.

 Jessica's Tip

There is a fair amount of detail in the paper template for this pie, but don't knock yourself out cutting out every little detail from the paper; it's enough to just get the outside shapes.

(continued on page 129)

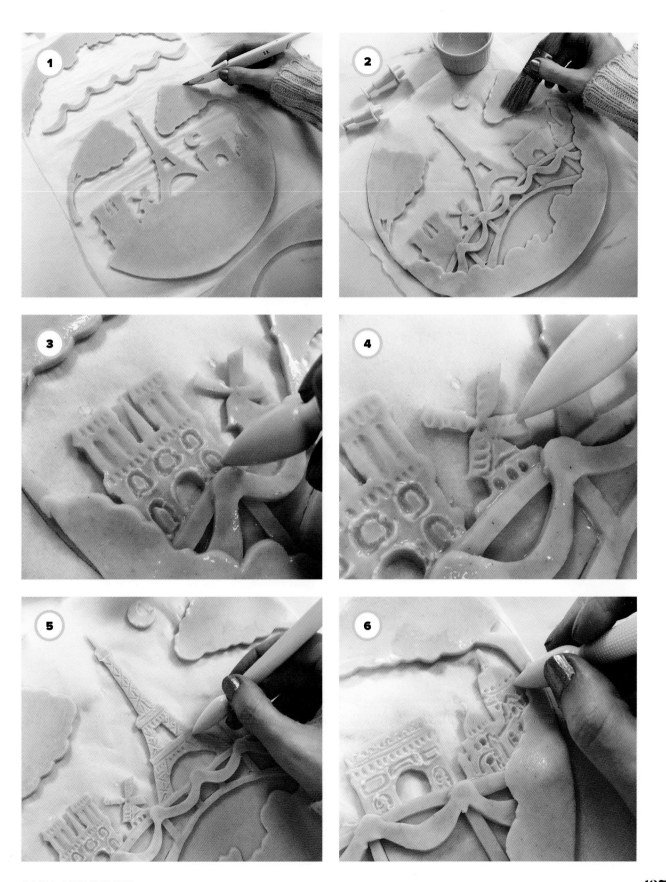

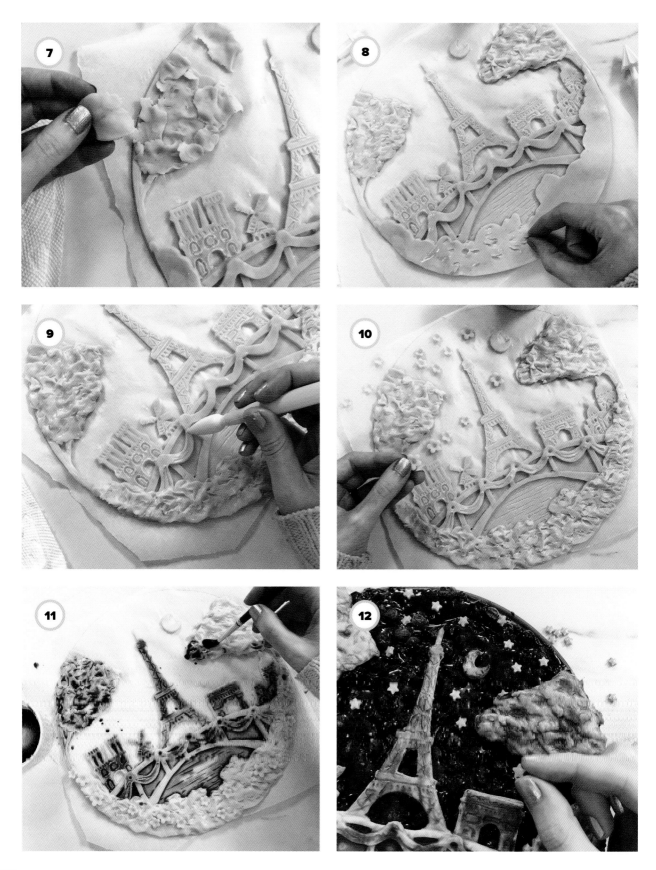

(continued from page 126)

7. When you've finished detailing the buildings, it's time to move on to the trees! First, coat them with some pasteurized egg whites, then score some tiny vertical grooves into the trunks to emulate bark. For the treetops, pinch little bits of the dough with your fingernails to create the impression of lumpy leaves. If the treetops start to get too thin, feel free to add some extra dough bits on top before you start with your fingernail "smooshing."

8. Coat the shrubbery in pasteurized egg whites, then use your fingernails to pinch little bits of the dough to create the impression of lumpy leaves, like you did with the treetops. Because the shrubbery is sitting on top of a couple layers of dough already, you should have plenty to work with there.

9. Score curved lines into the banners on the bridge with the fondant sculpting tool, to give them a sense of volume.

10. This is an optional step, but I added some flowers cut out with the small flower-shaped plunger cutters to the bottom of my pie, on top of the shrubbery. They may not look completely "realistic," but I think it makes for an interesting composition!

11. Once all the details are complete, use the food-safe artist brush to give everything a generous vanilla wash with a mixture of vanilla extract and a little brown gel food color, making sure the mixture seeps into all the cracks. Carefully place the parchment paper with your skyline onto the baking sheet and bake at 400°F (200°C; gas mark 6) for 10 to 14 minutes, or until golden brown.

Pie-Modding Ideas

Does your family have a special relationship to another country? Why not try creating your own city skyline pie in honor of that city? Just Google the names of your favorite landmarks from that city with the word "silhouette," then trace the buildings to size for your pie. All you need is a foreground layer, which could be a bridge, shrubs, water, or anything else relevant to the city; a mid-ground layer, which could include monuments; and a background layer, which could be mountains, clouds, trees, or just a beautiful sunset made of different colors of filling or sanding sugar. A city skyline pie would make a delightful gift for the elders in your family, especially when paired with flavors from the "old country"!

12. While your skyline is cooling, bake your base pie. As soon as the base pie comes out of the oven, bubbling hot, carefully place the skyline on top with the cake lifter. The hot filling will fuse the top and bottom together as if they were baked together! Finish off your pie by adding the gold star sprinkles to the blueberry night sky. Use the hashtags #SkylinePie and #PiesAreAwesomeTheBook when you post pics of your version of this pie—I'd love to see what you create!

Mandala Pie

Diwali is a festival of lights celebrated in late autumn by people of Hindu, Sikh, and other faiths. There is a rich history behind this beautiful festival, and I encourage you to do some research into the myriad meanings behind the occasion, but at a high level, you can think of Diwali as a celebration of the symbolic victory of "light over darkness" and "knowledge over ignorance," depicted through breathtaking displays of lights and color and enjoyed with loved ones. This pie is my humble homage to the Rangoli sand mandalas, which I figured was fitting, given that they are both temporary artistic mediums!

Level: Intermediate

Ingredients

+ Dough of your choice for 1½ double-crust pies
+ Pasteurized egg whites (or almond milk if making a vegan pie)
+ Vanilla extract
+ Brown gel food color
+ Gel food colors of your choice
+ Sanding sugar colors of your choice
+ Gold and pearl luster dusts (optional)
+ Vodka (or any clear alcohol or extract to mix with the luster dusts) (optional)
+ Assortment of nonpareils and sugar pearls (optional)

Supplies

+ Parchment paper
+ Rolling pin
+ Ramekins or small containers to hold pasteurized egg whites and mix color
+ Pastry brush
+ Paper templates
+ Food-safe precision blade
+ Assorted small flower- and geometric-shaped cutters (optional)
+ Fondant sculpting tool (or toothpick)
+ Food-safe artist brushes
+ Toothpicks (for gel food colors)
+ Baking sheet
+ Pie pan of your choice
+ Cake lifter

Dough of Your Choice
You can use cookie-style, all-butter, all-shortening, all-lard, half-and-half, or vegan dough interchangeably. Puff pastry is the only dough that may cause overly extreme distortions.

Base Pie
Create a base pie with a decorative crimped edge and the filling of your choice. Consider mango, coconut, pistachio, and ghee for a modern twist on traditional Diwali flavors!

Resources
For instructions on downloading and printing the template for this pie, go to page 206. For edge-crimping suggestions, see page 60.

Jessica's Tip

Consider opting for a slightly tart filling or one with no added sweetener because you will be adding sanding sugar. Apple, peach, or mango without extra sugar can be great options, or try coconut-based cream pies or mousses for a different texture!

1. Roll out two layers of pie dough, each ⅛ inch (3 mm) thick, on a piece of parchment paper with your rolling pin. Give what will be the bottom layer of dough a wash of pasteurized egg whites with a pastry brush, and then carefully place the second layer on top and pat it down. Place the large template on the dough and cut out the main shape of your mandala from both layers of dough with your food-safe precision blade.

2. Using the smaller paper templates, cut out the interior mandala shapes through the top layer of dough only.

3. Using your precision blade as a tiny spatula, carefully lift up and remove alternative sections of the top layer of dough and set them aside.

4. Now it's time to add some detail! Starting in the center, cut out a flower shape, then cut out the smaller shapes in a radiating pattern around the flower. (If you have flower- and geometric-shaped cutters on hand, you can use those in place of the templates.) Reserve the cutout shapes.

5. Paste the reserved cutout shapes around the perimeter of your mandala with pasteurized egg whites.

6. Coat the entire mandala with pasteurized egg whites. Using the fondant sculpting tool, add some extra little details to amp up the visual interest. They can be hand-rolled dough balls, tiny shapes you cut out with your own cutters, or additional instances of the paper template shapes.

(continued on page 135)

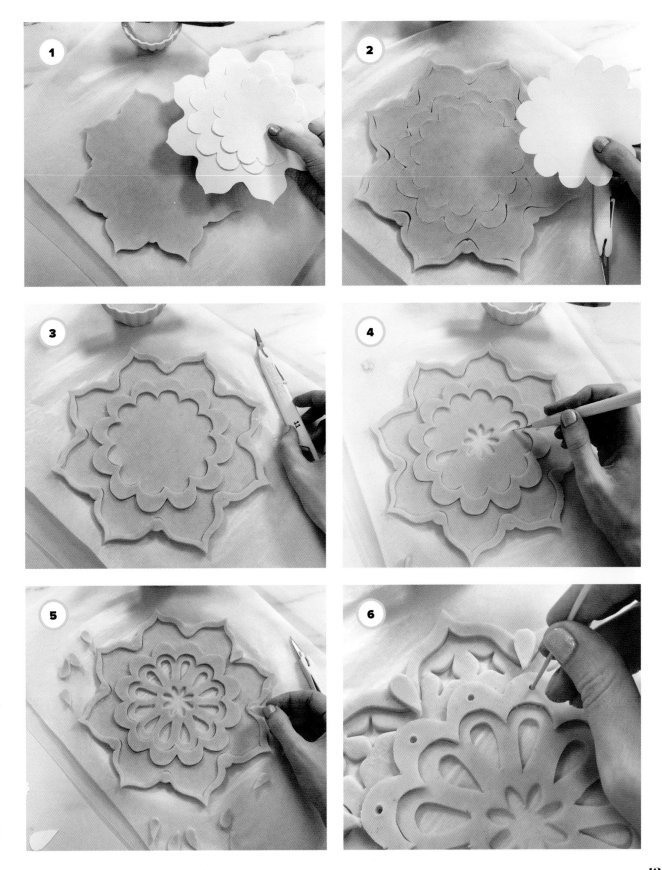

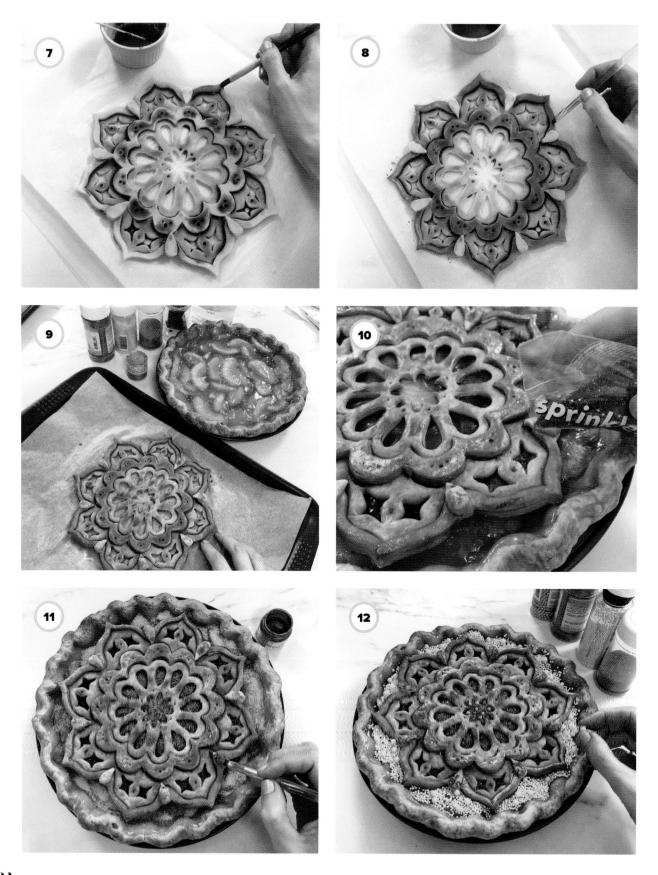

(continued from page 132)

 Jessica's Tip

There's a trick to cutting out or placing decorations that you would like to be evenly spaced around a circle. Think of your dough circle like a clockface. If you were asked to place the numbers on a clockface freehand, you would most likely start with the numbers 12 and 6, which are directly across from each other. Once you are fairly certain you have put them in the correct place, you can then place the numbers 3 and 9, and then fill in the remaining numbers with confidence that those first "anchor" placements are correct!

7. Once you are happy with your mandala design, use a food-safe artist brush to give your dough a vanilla wash with vanilla extract mixed with a tiny bit of brown gel food color, making sure the mixture seeps into the cracks.

8. Paint your mandala the colors of your choice using gel food colors mixed with vanilla extract. (Add 1½ teaspoons of vanilla extract to a ramekin, then dab a generous toothpick full of gel color on the edge of the ramekin. Dip your food-safe artist brush into the vanilla and then into the pigment on the side and paint away!) Try to leave some areas unpainted so that the natural color of the dough will shine through! This lets people know that it is, in fact, delicious pastry that they are about to eat—and it helps you know when your dough is done in the oven. Once you have finished painting, carefully place the parchment paper with your mandala onto a baking sheet and bake at 400°F (200°C; gas mark 6) for about 12 minutes, or until golden brown.

9. While your mandala is cooling, bake your base pie with a crimped edge. As soon as your base pie comes out of the oven, bubbling hot, carefully place your mandala on top with the cake lifter.

10. Let the pie cool for an hour, and then add sanding sugar to the exposed-filling areas for some extra pops of color and to get that Rangoli sand effect.

11. You can also paint some areas of the crust design with luster dust mixed with a few drops of vodka, if desired. Just remember that a little luster dust goes a long way!

12. If you are feeling extra blingy (and who wouldn't be?), you can add some sprinkles of different sizes and shapes to finish it off. Use the hashtags #MandalaPie and #PiesAreAwesomeTheBook when you post pics of your version of this pie—I'd love to see what you create!

Pie-Modding Ideas

There are so many design possibilities with mandala pies! All you need is a paper background template that is smaller than your pie pan and a handful of little cutter shapes to add the cutout details. Try creating your paper background template the same way you create a paper snowflake! Just Google "simple paper mandala" for a ton of neat ideas.

Chibi Pumpkin Pie

It's chibi time! What's "chibi," you ask? Well, in a nutshell, it's a Japanese word meaning "short and chubby," but it has come to refer to anything extra cute with baby-like features—big eyes, big forehead, rosy cheeks, all that good stuff. Here I've applied it to a simple jack-o'-lantern design to create a super cute, and super easy, Halloween pie. In fact, it's so super easy, you don't even have to bake the pie yourself if you don't want to! You can still be the hero of the Halloween party by picking up a store-bought pie and a roll of prefab dough and adding the face and sprinkles yourself. A 15-minute pie hack . . . don't tell me "ain't nobody got time for that!"

Level: Beginner

Ingredients

- ✦ Dough of your choice for 1 double-crust pie
- ✦ Pasteurized egg whites (or almond milk if making a vegan pie)
- ✦ Vanilla extract
- ✦ Brown gel food color
- ✦ Black, green, and pink gel food colors
- ✦ Opaque white icing color
- ✦ Orange and yellow sanding sugar

Supplies

- ✦ Parchment paper
- ✦ Rolling pin
- ✦ Paper templates
- ✦ Food-safe precision blade
- ✦ Ramekins or small containers to hold pasteurized egg whites and mix color
- ✦ Pastry brush
- ✦ Fondant sculpting tool (or toothpick)
- ✦ Toothpicks (for gel food colors)
- ✦ Food-safe artist brushes
- ✦ Baking sheet
- ✦ Pie pan of your choice
- ✦ Metal spatula (optional)

Dough of Your Choice

For this pie, you can use cookie, gluten-free, rough puff, all-butter, or vegan dough interchangeably.

I used a store-bought roll-out crust. You can even use an already baked store-bought base pie and save yourself some time!

Base Pie

Create a base pie with a decorative crimped edge. This pie is a literal picture of a pumpkin, so I think it makes sense for the filling to be pumpkin, but then again, who am I to stifle your creativity? Because this pie has a sanding sugar top, you can use any flavor of filling you like, though you may want to use something that isn't overly sweet and possibly even tart.

Resources

For instructions on downloading and printing the template for this pie, go to page 206. For edge-crimping suggestions, see page 60.

1. Roll out your dough ⅛ inch (3 mm) thick on a piece of parchment paper with your rolling pin. Place the template pieces and cut out all the shapes with your food-safe precision blade.

2. Coat the pieces in pasteurized egg whites with the pastry brush. While the dough is still wet, use the fondant sculpting tool to score some lines on the stem and leaf.

3. Paste the leaf to the stem with pasteurized egg whites, then cut out three thin strips of dough to make vines. Coat these in pasteurized egg whites and coil them around the stem and leaf in whatever way floats your boat. I made a little curlicue with one of mine because it reminded me of baby doll hair!

4. Mix your black, green, and pink gel food colors with vanilla extract and paint your pieces. (Add 1½ teaspoons of vanilla extract to a ramekin, then dab a generous toothpick full of gel color on the edge of the ramekin. Dip your food-safe artist brush into the vanilla and then into the pigment on the side and paint away!) If the filling of your pie is quite dark, consider painting the face bits yellow, or even just leaving them unpainted. If the filling background is bright, like my sanding-sugar design, then choose a dark color, like black. I paint the stem green and the cheeks pink. To make the stem look a little more "natural," I gave it a quick wash with a more diluted green color (more vanilla extract and less pigment) to let some of the natural dough show through. Finally, add

some shine to the eyes with the white icing color. Carefully place the parchment paper with your pumpkin pieces onto a baking sheet and bake at 400°F (200°C; gas mark 6) for about 8 minutes.

5. While your pumpkin pieces are cooling, bake your base pie with a crimped edge. Flatten down about 2 inches (5 cm) at the top of the trim to accommodate the stem. If you are using a store-bought pie, break off a little bit of the trim so that the stem can lie flat.

6. Once your base pie has cooled and you are ready to serve it, add your sanding sugar. I've made a bit of an ombre effect with yellow at the top fading to orange at the bottom, but you do you! A solid color will look cool too. Finally, add the face and stem with your hands or a metal spatula. To get the true chibi effect, place the eyes below the center line of the face. Use the hashtags #ChibiPumpkinPie and #PiesAreAwesomeTheBook when you post pics of your version of this pie—I'd love to see what you create!

Pie-Modding Ideas

This is such a simple pie design, yet surprisingly versatile with just a few tweaks. Swap out the stem on top for some bunny ears, and you've got yourself a Chibi Easter Bunny pie! Or change the little triangle nose and mouth into a big red circle, throw in some tiny antlers, and now it's a Rudolph pie! Or maybe try some little bear ears or kitty whiskers, or turn your crust trim into a lion mane. There's no limit to the adorable critters you can concoct with this design. Which chibi face will most delight the kids (or grown-up kids) in your life?

Monster Mouth Pie

One of my favorite parts of Halloween is getting to spend time on fun, creative projects with my young son—from costume making and decorating the house and porch to whipping up spooky-themed treats! This Monster Mouth Pie was actually his idea, and he did all the work creating the first iteration back when he was six years old (I was just on hand to do the cutting out and oven parts). He was so proud of the finished product. You can actually watch the video of us making it together on my featured Story on Instagram! I hope you and your monster-loving munchkins have as much fun baking this pie together as we did.

Level: Beginner

Ingredients

+ Dough of your choice for 1 double-crust pie
+ Pasteurized egg whites (or almond milk if making a vegan pie)
+ Vanilla extract
+ Brown gel food color
+ Opaque white icing color
+ Black gel food color

Supplies

+ Parchment paper
+ Rolling pin
+ Pie pan of your choice
+ Food-safe precision blade
+ Bowl, plate, or cup, roughly 4 to 5 inches (10 to 12.5 cm) in diameter
+ Ramekins or small containers to hold pasteurized egg whites and mix color
+ Pastry brush
+ Spoon
+ Paper templates
+ Food-safe artist brushes
+ Toothpicks
+ Baking sheet
+ Cake lifter

Dough of Your Choice

For this pie you can use pretty much any dough. The design elements are simple, so it really doesn't matter if they puff up and distort a bit. We used store-bought dough just to make things simpler.

Base Pie

Create an infinity-edge base pie with the filling extending all the way to the edges (see page 60). For our initial base pie, my son wanted an "every flavor pie," so we mixed three different cans of pie fillings together . . . I'm not sure if I recommend that strategy, but as long as you choose a dark-colored filling, it will create a nice contrast for the mouth!

Resources

For instructions on downloading and printing the template for this pie, go to page 206.

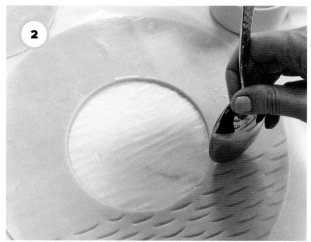

1. Roll out your dough on a piece of parchment paper with your rolling pin. Lay your pie pan facedown on the rolled-out dough and cut out a circle the size of your pie pan with your food-safe precision blade. Place the bowl, plate, or cup in the center of your dough circle and cut out a second circle from the middle. Set this cutout piece aside; you will use this piece of dough to cut out your details later.

2. Coat the large dough circle again with a generous helping of pasteurized egg whites with the pastry brush, then starting from the bottom, gently mark little "scales" with the tip of the spoon.

3. Place the templates for the eyes, eyebrows, hands, feet, and teeth on the piece of dough you set aside and cut out the shapes.

4. Coat the large circle of dough with pasteurized egg whites, then paste the features onto your pie wherever your tiny art-director commands. Don't worry about making it look just like mine! The wonkier the better when it comes to crazy monster pies.

5. Use a food-safe artist brush to give the whole monster a vanilla wash with vanilla extract mixed with a tiny bit of brown gel food color, making sure the mixture seeps into the cracks. Paint the eyes with the white color icing, the eyebrows with the brown gel food color mixed with vanilla extract, and the pupils with the black gel food color mixed with vanilla extract. (Add 1½ teaspoons of vanilla extract to a ramekin, then dab a generous toothpick full of gel color on the edge of the ramekin. Dip your food-safe artist brush into the vanilla and then into the pigment on the side and paint away!) Or use whatever colors you want! Maybe your monster wants to have green eyes and purple eyebrows? Who am I to judge?

6. Carefully place the parchment paper with your monster onto a baking sheet and bake for 10 to 12 minutes at 400°F (200°C; gas mark 6), or until golden brown. While your monster top is cooling, bake your base pie with an infinity edge. As soon as your base pie comes out of the oven, bubbling hot, carefully place your monster on top with the cake lifter. Lightly press down for 5 seconds so that the top and base fuse together. Use the hashtags #MonsterMouthPie and #PiesAreAwesomeTheBook when you post pics of your version of this pie—I'd love to see what you create!

✶ Jessica's Tip ✶

Turn your pie into a fun interactive game at the end by "teeding" your monster grapes, chocolate chips, marshmallows, or any small edible item that would go well with the flavor of your filling! With my son and my original pie, we took turns trying to throw eyeball sprinkles into his mouth and hilarity ensued. Yes, we were picking eyeball sprinkles out of the carpet for a week, but it was totally worth it for the giggles and memories!

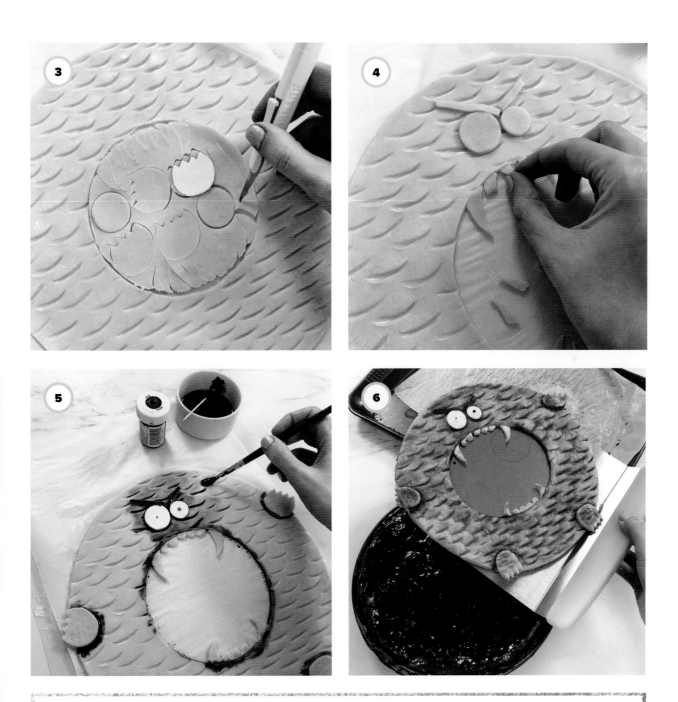

Pie-Modding Ideas

You can use this general design for any style of critter with a big mouth. I made a Bowser pie using this concept (you can find it on my Instagram @ThePieous), but Kirby, JigglyPuff, or even just miscellaneous creatures, like a big-mouthed bunny, would be fun too!

La Catrina Pie

This is one of my favorite pie designs, and it makes me wish that it was socially acceptable to make spooky things year-round! This pie design features my take on La Catrina, Mexico's good-natured Grand Dame of Death, who presides over Día de los Muertos festivals. Far from being "Mexican Halloween," the Day of the Dead is a time for honoring loved ones who have passed on with beautiful shrines filled with marigold flowers and all that loved one's favorite things—including food!

Level: Advanced

Ingredients

+ Dough of your choice for 1½ double-crust pies
+ Pasteurized egg whites (or almond milk if making a vegan pie)
+ Brown gel food color
+ Vanilla extract
+ Orange, yellow, and pink gel food colors (or colors of your choice)
+ Gold and pearl luster dusts
+ Vodka (or any clear alcohol or extract to mix with the luster dusts)
+ Edible adhesive (such as jam or sugar glue)
+ Some sort of edible "crunch" for the exposed pie edges (sprinkles, crushed nuts, cereal bits, coarse brown sugar, etc.) (optional)

Supplies

+ Parchment paper
+ Flexible cutting mats
+ Rolling pin
+ Paper templates
+ Food-safe precision blade
+ Ramekins or small containers to hold pasteurized egg whites and mix color
+ Pastry brush
+ Assorted flower-shaped punches, plunger cutters, or molds (optional)
+ Fondant sculpting tool (or toothpick)
+ Food-safe artist brushes
+ Toothpicks (for the gel food colors)
+ Baking sheet
+ Pie pan of your choice
+ Cake lifter

Dough of Your Choice

Because this is a more detailed pie, I suggest sticking with the cookie-style doughs, store-bought roll-out crust, or a shortening-based shortcrust dough to minimize puffiness.

Base Pie

Create an infinity-edge base pie with the filling extending all the way to the edges (see page 60). Any flavor will do!

Resources

For instructions on downloading and printing the template for this pie, go to page 206.

  Jessica's Tip

Why not create your Day of the Dead pie in honor of someone special in your life and choose filling flavors that reference their favorite foods?

1. Roll out a piece of your dough ⅛ inch (3 mm) thick on a parchment-lined flexible cutting mat with your rolling pin. Place the template of the main head shape on the rolled-out dough and cut out the shape with your food-safe precision blade. Remove the template and give the dough a generous coating of pasteurized egg whites with the pastry brush. Set the dough scraps aside to use later.

2. Roll out a second piece of dough ⅛ inch (3 mm) thick on a parchment-lined flexible cutting mat, lay down the skull and jaw templates, and cut out the shapes. Poke guide holes through the eyes and nose shapes with the precision blade.

3. Remove the templates and cut out the eyes and nose, using the guide holes as a cutting reference. Paste the skull and jaw onto the main head shape with pasteurized egg whites.

4. Cut out all the decorative scrolly shapes and paste them on the head and neck with pasteurized egg whites. If you are having trouble cutting the small details, try chilling your dough in the freezer for 2 minutes first. (If you have your own cutter shapes or molds, you can use those in place of the templates.)

5. Coat all the dough in pasteurized egg whites again, then use the fondant sculpting tool to score extra swirly lines and dots into the dough until you are happy with the final design.

6. Set your dough head in the fridge for a moment on its parchment-lined flexible cutting mat and roll some small balls from the spare dough to make the tiny sugar skulls that will adorn La Catrina's hair. Start by rolling the dough into spheres with your hands, then pinch the bottoms to make a little wedge shape. Coat the shapes in pasteurized egg whites, then, using your fondant sculpting tool, poke two holes for eyes, a line for the mouth, and a series of tiny holes for the teeth.

★ Jessica's Tip ★

Don't feel obligated to use all the template shapes! If you are finding it too fiddly to cut around all the small shapes and don't have any cutters or molds, consider scoring your swirly lines with the fondant sculpting tool instead of placing dough appliqués on top. It will be a slightly different look, but still detailed and cool!

(continued on page 149)

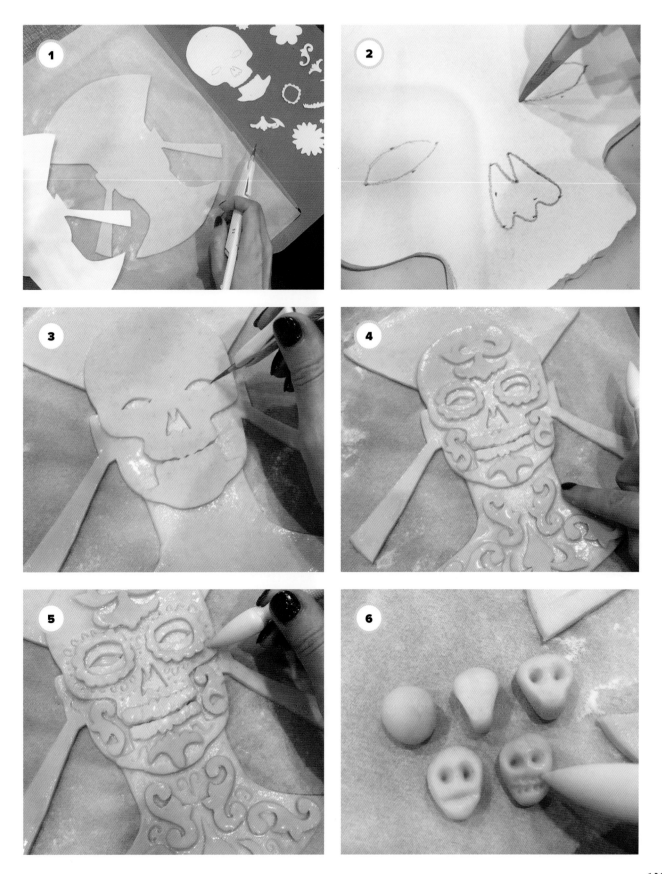

(continued from page 146)

7. Now it's flower-power time! Using the paper templates provided or your own molds and cutters, cut out an assortment of flowers to adorn our lady's hair.

8. Coat the flowers in pasteurized egg whites and add some simple scored details to the flowers as pictured, then paste them above the face. Remember that your dough cannot be more than three layers thick or it will not bake fully! If you want to layer your flowers more densely, bake a few of them separately on a baking sheet and then paste them on with a bit of leftover pie filling at the end.

9. Paint the neck and face dark brown with your gel food color mixed with vanilla extract. (Add 1½ teaspoons of vanilla extract to a ramekin, then dab a generous toothpick full of gel color on the edge of the ramekin. Dip your food-safe artist brush into the vanilla and then into the pigment on the side and paint away!) Be careful not to get any color on the added decorations or other parts of the dough that you would like to remain unpainted.

10. Use a food-safe artist brush to give the little skulls, the flowers in the crown, and the rays emanating from her head a vanilla wash with a mixture of vanilla extract and a tiny bit of brown gel food color.

11. Add some color to the flowers now with the gel food colors mixed with vanilla extract—orange, yellow, and pink are traditional Day of the Dead colors, but feel free to throw in some purple, teal, or whatever floats your boat!

12. Carefully place the parchment paper with your La Catrina onto the baking sheet and bake at 400°F (200°C; gas mark 6) for about 14 minutes, or until the unpainted parts are golden brown. As soon as your base pie comes out of the oven, bubbling hot, carefully place your La Catrina on top with the cake lifter. Once your La Catrina has cooled, you can add some extra bling to the flowers with a bit of the luster dusts mixed with a few drops of vodka and paste on the little skulls with the edible adhesive. Add the "crunch" to the exposed edges to finish it off. Use the hashtags #DayoftheDeadPie and #PiesAreAwesomeTheBook when you post pics of your version of this pie—I'd love to see what you create!

Pie-Modding Ideas

For a Halloween-y twist, paint the skull white, nix the colorful flowers, and opt instead for a crown of spooky shapes, like spiders, bats, and twigs!

Goofy Turkey Pie

Thanksgiving feast preparations can be serious business—there's a lot of pressure to make everyone's favorite dishes just right. But sometimes it's worth deviating just a little from expectations and injecting some fun into the process. Imagine the delight on the kids' faces when you present your famous pumpkin or sweet potato pie at the end of the meal with this cheeky twist! (And the kids at heart might just love it too.)

Level: Beginner

Ingredients

+ Dough recipe of your choice to make a double-crust pie
+ Pasteurized egg whites (or almond milk if making a vegan pie)
+ Brown gel food color
+ Vanilla extract
+ Orange, red, yellow, and black gel food colors (or colors of your choice) (optional)
+ Opaque white icing color

Supplies

+ Rolling pin
+ Parchment paper
+ Paper templates
+ Food-safe precision blade
+ Ramekins or small containers to hold pasteurized egg whites and mix color
+ Pastry brush
+ Fondant sculpting tool (or toothpick)
+ Food-safe artist brushes
+ Toothpicks (optional)
+ Baking sheet
+ Pie pan of your choice
+ Metal spatula

Dough of Your Choice

You can use any type of dough with the exception of puff pastry. All-butter dough will distort the design slightly, but there's no harm if your goofy turkey looks a little goofier!

Base Pie

Create a base pie with a decorative crimped edge. A filling like pumpkin, sweet potato, or chess makes a good background for this design.

Resources

For instructions on downloading and printing the template for this pie, go to page 206. For edge-crimping suggestions, see page 60.

1. Roll out your dough ⅛ inch (3 mm) thick on a piece of parchment paper with your rolling pin. Place the templates on the rolled-out dough and cut out the shapes with your food-safe precision blade. Remove the templates and the excess dough.

2. Coat all the pieces in pasteurized egg whites with the pastry brush, and then use the fondant sculpting tool to add some details to the feathers.

3. Use a food-safe artist brush to give all the pieces a vanilla wash with a mixture of vanilla extract and a tiny bit of brown gel food color, making sure the mixture seeps into all the cracks.

4. At this point, you can keep the pieces unpainted or paint them with the gel food colors mixed with vanilla extract. (Add 1½ teaspoons of vanilla extract to a ramekin, then dab a generous toothpick full of gel color on the edge of the ramekin. Dip your food-safe artist brush into the vanilla and then into the pigment on the side and paint away!) I painted the feathers and feet with brown, orange, red, and yellow gel food colors and used white icing color for the eyes and black gel food color for the pupils. When you are happy

✷ Jessica's Tip ✷

Even if you choose to keep the rest of the pieces unpainted, it is a good idea to paint the turkey's eyeballs white with the white icing color, as dough-colored eyeballs will make your turkey look a bit . . . ahem . . . under the influence. Don't forget to add the pupils with black gel food color!

with the color, carefully place the parchment paper with your turkey's features onto the baking sheet and bake at 400°F (200°C; gas mark 6) for 8 to 12 minutes, or until golden brown.

5. While your turkey's features cool, bake your base pie with a crimped edge. When the base pie is done, carefully place the features on it with the spatula, working from the feet up. They will naturally stick to the top of the pie for the first 10 minutes or so after it comes out of the oven.

6. Finally, place the top feathers at the top of the pie, sticking out at angles to create a bit of a 3-D effect. Use the hashtags #GoofyTurkeyPie and #PiesAreAwesomeTheBook when you post pics of your version of this pie—I'd love to see what you create!

Pie-Modding Ideas

Not into turkeys? Change up the nose shape and turn the top feathers into ears for a goofy pig,
bunny, or bear cub!

Harvest Tree Pie

This simple but striking design requires no food paint at all! The brown of the tree is created using ground cinnamon and the little peek-a-boo views of the filling showing through the leaf cutouts add another bit of contrasting color and interest. Our leafy tree design would be right at home on a Thanksgiving table or harvest-themed wedding buffet, or any crispy autumn day that could do with a slice of hot apple pie!

Level: Beginner

Ingredients

+ Dough of your choice for 1½ double-crust pies
+ Pasteurized egg whites (or almond milk if making a vegan pie)
+ Ground cinnamon (or an edible powder of your choice)
+ Whole egg wash

Supplies

+ Parchment paper
+ Rolling pin
+ Paper template
+ Food-safe precision blade
+ Fondant sculpting tool (or toothpick) (optional)
+ Pie pan of your choice
+ Ramekin or small container to hold pasteurized egg whites
+ Pastry brush
+ Offset spatula
+ Fork
+ Cake lifter

Dough of Your Choice

Great news! Any type of dough will work with this pie design—even puff pastry (it will be a pretty puffy tree, but it will still look like a tree).

Base Pie

This project and the Quilt Pie on page 111 are the only two projects in the book in which the top and bottom of the pie are combined and baked together with a decorative crimped edge. Your base pie can be any flavor you think will pair well with the spice topping you choose. I made a regular apple pie, but why not consider a mile-high apple pie?

 Jessica's Tip

I used ground cinnamon to pair with a sweet filling, but for a savory pie filling, try paprika or even ground nutmeg for a bit of exotic flair.

Resources

For instructions on downloading and printing the template for this pie, go to page 206. For edge-crimping suggestions, see page 60.

1. Roll out enough dough ⅛ inch (3 mm) thick on a piece of parchment with your rolling pin to fit the tree template. Place the tree template on the dough and cut out the shape with your food-safe precision blade. Remove the template.

2. Coat the tree shape in pasteurized egg whites with the pastry brush and sprinkle the ground cinnamon over the top. Tap it down with your fingers to ensure good adhesion, and then carefully brush off the excess powder.

3. Using your precision blade, score little lines up and down the tree to create the illusion of bark. (You can also use a fondant sculpting tool or a toothpick to do this.) Place the tree in the freezer to harden while you work on the rest of the pie.

4. Roll out some more dough ⅛ inch (3 mm) thick on a piece of parchment paper. Lay your pie pan facedown on the rolled-out dough and cut out a circle the size of your pie pan. Coat this dough circle in pasteurized egg whites with the pastry brush. Remove the tree from the freezer, and using the offset spatula, carefully place it on the dough circle.

5. With your precision blade, cut out little leaf shapes around the branches. Save the cutout shapes!

6. Paste the cutout leaf shapes around your branches with pasteurized egg whites until you

are happy with the look. Place the top decoration in the freezer. Now prepare your base pie as you would for a crimped-edge pie—roll out a sheet of dough 3 inches (7.5 cm) larger than your pie pan all around, transfer it to the pan, coat the bottom with egg wash, dock (poke) the dough with a fork, and add the filling. Remove the top decoration from the freezer and carefully place it on the center of your base pie with the cake lifter. Fold over the overhang of dough from the base pie to form a crimped edge. Cover the edges of your pie with foil and bake on a baking sheet at 400°F (200°C; gas mark 6) for 40 minutes. Remove the foil and add some egg wash to the crimped edges, then bake for another 20 minutes, or until the filling has been bubbling for 5 minutes. Use the hashtags #TreePie and #PiesAreAwesomeTheBook when you post pics of your version of this pie—I'd love to see what you create!

⭐ **Jessica's Tip** ⭐

Because you are baking your top decoration together with your base pie, you are going to get a bit of a filling explosion through the leaf holes. That's okay! This is a more rustic design, and a little imperfection will only make it more delicious.

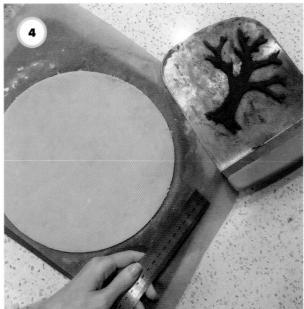

Pie-Modding Ideas

This cinnamon-on-a-cutout-shape concept can work with many different types of shapes. Why not try using cookie cutters you have on hand to create different compositions, like leaves, hearts, circles, or any small shape that can be formed in an interesting pattern? Or how about one giant powder-coated shape, like a huge snowflake or sunflower? You can also try using different colors of edible powders as an easy way to add a bit of interest and complexity.

Snowman Pie

Froooosty the pie mannn, was a jolly happy pieeee! Okay, I'm a pie maker, not a songwriter, but this happy little pie makes me feel like singing! It's such a simple concept too. Just place two pies with a white topping of some sort next to each other, and then plunk down some pie dough "cookies." It's easier than making a real snowman! This is also my son's favorite pie in the book, so you can add "kid approved" to the checklist of features.

Level: Beginner

Ingredients

+ Dough of your choice for 2 double-crust pies
+ Pasteurized egg whites (or almond milk if making a vegan pie)
+ Vanilla extract
+ Brown gel food color
+ Orange, red, black, and green gel food colors (or colors of your choice)
+ Green luster dust (or color of your choice) (optional)
+ Vodka (or any clear alcohol or extract to mix with the luster dust) (optional)
+ 2 cups (120 g) meringue (prepared from scratch or from a powder mix) or whipped topping

Supplies

+ Parchment paper
+ Rolling pin
+ Paper templates
+ Food-safe precision blade
+ Ramekins or small containers to hold pasteurized egg whites and mix color
+ Pastry brush
+ Fondant sculpting tool (or toothpick)
+ Food-safe artist brushes
+ Baking sheet
+ 2 tart or pie pans of different sizes
+ Large piping bag with a star tip
+ Cake lifter
+ Kitchen torch

Dough of Your Choice

I made this pie with the Sweet Pie Dough recipe on page 216, which has a cookie-like texture, but any dough that doesn't bake obscenely puffy (such as puff pastry) will do!

Base Pie

Create two tarts or pies of different sizes. If using pie pans, create pies with an infinity edge (see page 60). I used a store-bought mixture for a pink lemonade curd filling. You want something that will work well with a meringue topping.

Resources

For instructions on downloading and printing the template for this pie, go to page 206. For edge-crimping suggestions, see page 60.

1. Roll out your dough ⅛ inch (3 mm) thick on a piece of parchment paper with your rolling pin. Place all the templates on the rolled-out dough and cut out the shapes with your food-safe precision blade.

2. With a bit of pasteurized egg whites on your finger, smooth out the sharp edges of the cutout shapes to round them off and give them more of a three-dimensional appearance.

3. Brush some pasteurized egg whites onto the hat with the pastry brush, and then paste the band on the hat. Trim off any overhang with your precision blade.

4. Coat all the pieces in pasteurized egg whites with the pastry brush, and then use the fondant sculpting tool to score little "stitch" marks into the scarf piece. Indent a line between the horizontal top of the scarf and the vertical part pointing down so that it looks like the scarf is "wrapped" around the snowman's neck. Be careful not to score too deep or it will separate in the oven.

5. Poke holes through the buttons, score circles around the button perimeters, and score some curved lines around the carrot to make it look 3-D.

6. Use a food-safe artist brush to give all your pieces a vanilla wash with a mixture of vanilla extract and a tiny bit of brown gel food color, making sure the mixture seeps into all the cracks. Now paint the pieces with the gel food colors mixed with vanilla extract. (Add 1½ teaspoons of vanilla extract to a ramekin, then dab a generous toothpick full of gel color on the edge of the ramekin. Dip your food-safe artist brush into the vanilla and then into the pigment on the side and paint away!) I used orange for the carrot nose, red for the scarf, black for the hat and eyes, green for the buttons, and brown for the stick hands, as well as to highlight the details of the other pieces.)

(continued on page 163)

(continued from page 160)

7. Carefully place the parchment paper with your snowman's features onto the baking sheet and bake the at 350°F (175°C; gas mark 4) for 8 minutes if you are using the Sweet Pie Dough. If you are using any of the shortcrust doughs, bake at 400°F (200°C; gas mark 6) for 10 minutes. Once the pieces have baked, you can give the buttons a little coating of green luster dust mixed with a few drops of vodka if you desire.

8. While your snowman's features are cooling, bake your base pies. If using a filling similar to mine, you will need to blind-bake the shells before adding the filling (see page 226 and the Resources section on page 228 for instructions on how to blind-bake pie shells).

9. Cook the pie filling on the stove according to the instructions on the box of whatever filling you have chosen, pour it into your blind-baked shells, and let set.

10. Once the base pies are fully set and cooled, make the meringue (if not using whipped topping). Spoon it into the large piping bag with the star tip. Place your base pies where you are going to be serving them.

11. Pipe the meringue onto the pies, and then torch the meringue with the kitchen torch.

12. Finally, arrange the baked decorations on the pie. Use the hashtags #SnowmanPie and #PiesAreAwesomeTheBook when you post pics of your version of this pie—I'd love to see what you create!

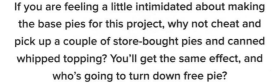

★ Jessica's Tip ★

If you are feeling a little intimidated about making the base pies for this project, why not cheat and pick up a couple of store-bought pies and canned whipped topping? You'll get the same effect, and who's going to turn down free pie?

Pie-Modding Ideas

This dual-pie concept is pretty versatile. Mix it up by swapping out the snowman decorations for Easter bunny ones, or turn these pies into a fluffy polar bear!

Gelt Pie

Though I am not Jewish myself, I have many friends and extended family members who are. As such, we often try to incorporate multiple faiths' celebrations into our winter holiday gatherings. For this pie, I wanted to bring in some of the flavors of the sufganiyot (a type of jelly doughnut) while also giving a nod to the gelt (chocolate coins wrapped in gold foil) that we play for in our dreidel games. It may not be a "traditional" Hanukkah dessert, but my family is all about the fusion of different beliefs and values, so it only makes sense to serve a fusion dessert!

Level: Beginner

Ingredients

+ Dough of your choice for 1 double-crust pie
+ Pasteurized egg whites (or almond milk if making a vegan pie)
+ Vanilla extract
+ Brown gel food color
+ Red sanding sugar

Supplies

+ Parchment paper
+ Rolling pin
+ Paper template
+ Food-safe precision blade
+ Stainless-steel ruler
+ Ramekins or small containers to hold pasteurized egg whites and mix vanilla wash
+ Pastry brush
+ Fondant sculpting tool (or toothpick)
+ Food-safe artist brush
+ Baking sheet
+ Pie pan of your choice
+ Cake lifter

Dough of Your Choice

Any dough will work for this pie design. I used an all-butter dough—as you can see, it is a little puffy after baking, but the basic shape is retained!

Jessica's Tip

If you are using a particularly puffy dough or a dough prone to spreading, freeze your top decoration overnight before baking to help retain sharper details.

Base Pie

Create a base pie with a decorative crimped edge. The traditional sufganiyot has a raspberry filling, but as long as you use any red filling, you'll get the same effect.

Resources

For instructions on downloading and printing the template for this pie, go to page 206. For edge-crimping suggestions, see page 60.

1. Roll out your dough ⅛ inch (3 mm) thick on a piece of parchment paper with your rolling pin. Lay your template on the dough and cut out the circle and interior shapes with your food-safe precision blade. Remove the template. Use your stainless-steel ruler to cut six strips around the long rectangular template piece.

2. Coat the dough circle in pasteurized egg whites with the pastry brush, and then paste the six strips to it to "outline" the Star of David. You can simply overlap the strips, or if you are feeling fancy, you can weave them together.

3. With the fondant sculpting tool, score little lines around the perimeter of the pie to emulate the edge of a coin.

4. Now score the lines for six decorative menorahs. Go around the circle, first scoring all the center branches and then the two bottom branches.

5. Add the remaining six branches to each menorah.

6. Use the food-safe artist brush to give the menorahs a vanilla wash with a mixture of vanilla extract and a tiny bit of brown gel food color, making sure the mixture seeps into all the cracks. Carefully place the parchment paper with your top decoration onto the baking sheet and bake at 400°F (200°C; gas mark 6) for 12 minutes, or until golden brown. While your top decoration cools, bake your base pie with a crimped edge. As soon as your base pie comes out of the oven, bubbling hot, carefully place your top decoration on top with the cake lifter. Finish off your design by sprinkling the exposed filling with the red sanding sugar. Use the hashtags #HanukkahPie and #PiesAreAwesomeTheBook when you post pics of your version of this pie—I'd love to see what you create!

Pie-Modding Ideas

If you have small Hanukkah-themed cookie cutters or stamps, you can use them to create the decorations around the dough circle instead of hand scoring the menorah design!

Sugar Plum Fairy Pie Doll

Pie dolls are pastry's answer to cake dolls, but without the plastic bits! Pie dolls are in the Piescraper family of pies, as they are intended to be viewed from the side rather than above. As such, they make a lovely holiday centerpiece, guaranteed to delight the kids . . . and at least mildly amuse the adults.

Level: Advanced

Ingredients

+ Dough of your choice for 1 double-crust pie
+ Pasteurized egg whites (or almond milk if making a vegan pie)
+ Opaque white icing color
+ Gel food colors of your choice
+ Vanilla extract
+ Luster dust colors of your choice
+ Vodka (or any clear alcohol or extract to mix with the luster dusts)
+ Sugar glue (such as Wilton Dab-N-Hold Edible Adhesive)
+ Sugar sheets or wafer paper
+ Scissors
+ White candy melts (optional)
+ 2 cups (120 g) meringue (prepared from scratch or from a powder mix)
+ Sugar pearls or dragées

Supplies

+ Parchment paper
+ Mini rolling pin
+ 4-inch (10 cm) tart ring (I like Silikomart brand) or 4- to 6-inch (10 to 15 cm) tart or pie pan
+ Perforated silicone baking mat (I like Silikomart's air mat)
+ Silikomart silicone impression strip
+ Stainless-steel ruler
+ Paper templates
+ Food-safe precision blade
+ Ramekins or small containers to hold pasteurized egg whites and mix color
+ Pastry brush
+ 6-inch (15 cm) lollipop stick
+ Fondant sculpting tool (or toothpick)
+ Food-safe artist brushes
+ Toothpicks (for the gel food colors)
+ Baking sheet
+ Metal spatula
+ Large piping bag with a star tip
+ Kitchen torch

Dough of Your Choice

I used the Sweet Pie Dough recipe on page 216 for this project, but I have also made pie dolls using store-bought and shortening-based doughs with great results. The cookie-style doughs will be easier for those of you not yet 100 percent confident with your shortcrust "standee" technique (see page 66).

Base Pie

While you can use any small base pie or tart for your pie doll, I have opted to create a special type of tart shell with Italian-style trim decoration and a pour-and-set filling.

Resources

For instructions on downloading and printing the template for this pie, go to page 206.

1. Roll out your dough ¼ inch (6 mm) thick on a piece of parchment paper with the mini rolling pin. Ready your tart ring, air mat, and silicone impression strip. OR simply roll out your dough into a tart or pie pan, bake the pie shell, and then skip ahead to step 8.

2. Using the silicone impression strip as a guide, cut out two pieces of dough with the stainless-steep ruler the exact width of the strip and long enough to make it at least halfway around the circumference of the tart ring.

3. Place the silicone impression strip inside the tart ring with the design facing inward, and then press a strip of dough firmly against it. This will thin out the dough strip somewhat, but that is okay because we started out with a ¼-inch-thick (6 mm) strip.

4. Place the second strip of dough inside the tart ring and use the ruler to cut through and join it to the adjacent dough strip by pressing lightly along the seam with your finger. Press this dough strip against the impression strip as well.

5. Using the tart ring as a cutter, cut a circle of dough from the rolled-out dough for the bottom of the tart.

6. Move the tart ring to the silicone mat and insert the dough circle you just cut out inside the ring to form the bottom of the tart. It will be slightly larger than the available space, so use your fingers to pinch a seal up and around the sides of the tart.

 Jessica's Tip

If this is your first time using sweet dough, do a test run first to learn how long it needs to bake in your particular oven. You may need a little more or less time depending on the age and model of your oven.

(continued on page 173)

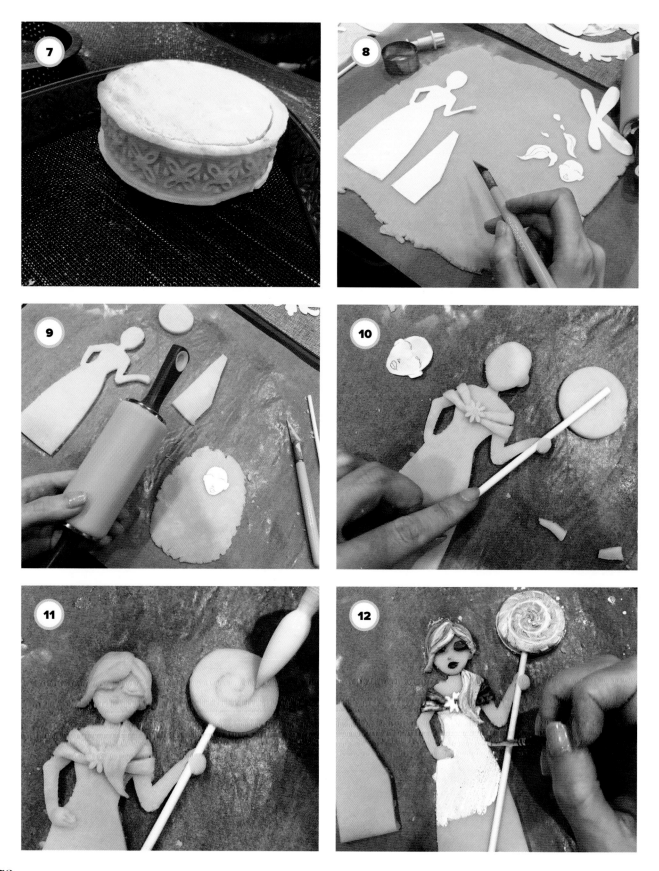

(continued from page 170)

7. Bake your tart shell at 350°F (175°C; gas mark 4) for 14 minutes, or until the dough is just beginning to lightly brown at the edge. Once your shell has baked, carefully remove the metal ring. The silicone impression strip should spring off by itself. At this point, if your tart shell is still slightly underbaked, you can cover the edge in foil and bake a couple minutes longer.

8. Now it's time for the doll! Roll out some more of your dough ¼ inch (6 mm) thick on a piece of parchment paper. Place the templates for the main body of the doll, the circle for the lollipop (cut out two), and the triangular "standee" support prop on the rolled-out dough and cut out the shapes with your food-safe precision blade. Set the wings template (pictured) aside for a later step.

9. With the mini rolling pin, flatten a piece of scrap dough to ⅛ inch (3 mm) thick. Place the templates of the doll features and details on this dough and cut out the shapes.

10. Coat the doll body in pasteurized egg whites with the pastry brush, and then paste the features and details on, lightly tapping them down. Position one of the lollipop circles and the lollipop stick, and then curl the doll's hand around the stick. Top the exposed stick with the other lollipop circle. Add a bit of scrap dough over the bottom end of the lollipop stick to help lock it in place. Don't worry; this part will be hidden by the meringue "skirt."

11. Using the fondant sculpting tool, score a swirled line into the lollipop, as well as lines along the doll's eyelashes, hair around her face, and ponytail.

12. Paint the doll with the white icing color and gel food colors mixed with vanilla extract. (Add 1½ teaspoons of vanilla extract to a ramekin, then dab a generous toothpick full of gel color on the edge of the ramekin. Dip your food-safe artist brush into the vanilla and then into the pigment on the side and paint away!) You do not need to paint the entire skirt because most of it will be hidden by the piped meringue. Carefully place the parchment paper with your doll and support prop onto the baking sheet and bake at 350°F (175°C; gas mark 4) for 10 minutes. Set aside to completely cool. At this point you may add some shimmery accents with a bit of the luster dusts mixed with a few drops of vodka.

> ### ✦ Jessica's Tip ✦
>
> This particular Pie Doll is done up in purples and pinks, as she is a Sugar Plum Fairy, but if you'd like a more traditional Christmassy spin, you can use red and gold or silver instead.

(continued on page 174)

(continued from page 173)

13. Once the pieces have cooled, paste the support prop into the tart shell using the sugar glue.

14. Cut out some fairy wings from the sugar sheets or wafer paper with scissors using the paper template as a guide. Add a dot of sugar glue to the center.

15. Carefully lift your cooled doll with a metal spatula and glue her in place with sugar glue in the tart shell, then place the wings on her back. Use whatever props you have on hand to help keep her upright while the adhesive sets. If anything should break off of your doll, use melted white candy melts to patch her back together.

16. While she is setting up, make your pie filling. Any type of pour-and-set filling that you can add to your pre-baked tart shell will do.

17. Once the filling is set in the tart shell, make the meringue and spoon it into the large piping bag with the star tip. Pipe a layer of meringue around the bottom of the doll's skirt and hit it with the kitchen torch. This will ensure that the skirt maintains its height and does not sink down into the filling as the pie sits out on the table for hours.

18. Pipe the meringue around the rest of the skirt and torch it. Add the sugar pearls or the bling of your choice to complete her outfit. Use the hashtags #PieDoll and #PiesAreAwesomeTheBook when you post pics of your version of this pie—I'd love to see what you create!

 Jessica's Tip

If you don't want to do a pour-and-set filling, and would rather have your Pie Doll embedded in a traditional filling pie, simply prepare your base pie as usual (with filling and shell baked together). Let it fully cool, and then use a knife to cut two slots through the filling perpendicular to each other for the doll and support prop to slide in.

Pie-Modding Ideas

If you find the creation of the doll portion of the project a bit too ambitious, you can always substitute a cardboard cutout of a figure glued to a toothpick. Then you can print out images of your favorite licensed characters and serve an assortment of little tart dresses at your next princess party. Take that, cupcakes!

Santa Claus Pie

This is a fun one! I'm always a big fan of using mixed media to create new and unexpected effects in the world of pastry arts, and my friends and family found the meringue of Santa's beard just delightful—and delicious! I've listed this as an "intermediate" pie because there are a fair number of steps, but each step is pretty simple, so feel free to give it a bash, even if you are a baking noob.

Level: Intermediate

Ingredients

+ Dough of your choice for 1½ double-crust pies
+ Pasteurized egg whites (or almond milk if making a vegan pie)
+ Vanilla extract
+ Brown gel food color
+ Red, pink, and black gel food colors
+ Opaque white icing color
+ 1 cup (60 g) meringue (prepared from scratch or from a powder mix)
+ Pink sanding sugar

Supplies

+ Parchment paper
+ Rolling pin
+ Pie pan of your choice
+ Food-safe precision blade
+ 1- to 2-inch (2.5 to 5 cm) round cookie cutter
+ Stainless-steel ruler
+ Fondant sculpting tool (or toothpick)
+ Paper templates
+ Ramekins or small containers to hold pasteurized egg whites and mix color
+ Pastry brush
+ Food-safe artist brushes
+ Toothpicks (for the gel food colors)
+ Baking sheet
+ Cake lifter
+ Large piping bag with a star tip
+ Kitchen torch

Dough of Your Choice

For this pie you can use cookie-style, all-shortening, all-lard, or half-and-half dough interchangeably. I used the Vegan Pie Dough recipe on page 214.

Base Pie

Create an infinity-edge base pie with the filling extending all the way to the edges (see page 60). Any type of filling will work!

Resources

For instructions on downloading and printing the template for this pie, go to page 206.

1. Roll out a full-size sheet of dough ⅛ inch (3 mm) thick on a piece of parchment paper with your rolling pin. Lay your pie pan facedown on the rolled-out dough and cut out a circle the size of your pie pan with your food-safe precision blade.

2. Using the round cookie cutter and the stainless-steel ruler to cut them in half, cut out enough semicircles to go all the way around the perimeter of your dough circle.

3. Coat the large dough circle in pasteurized egg whites with the pastry brush and paste the semicircles down around the perimeter. Use the fondant sculpting tool to score a line from the center of the semicircles down to the dough circle. This not only adds a decorative touch, but also helps adhere the two layers together.

4. Place the Santa head template on your dough and very lightly score a line around the outside of the shape with the fondant sculpting tool. Remove the template.

5. Cut out the remaining template shapes from a second piece of dough with your precision blade.

6. Coat all the dough pieces in pasteurized egg whites, then paste down the eyes, mouth, hat, and pom-pom on the dough circle. Cut out Santa's cheeks completely and remove the dough—the pie filling will show through here.

(continued on page 181)

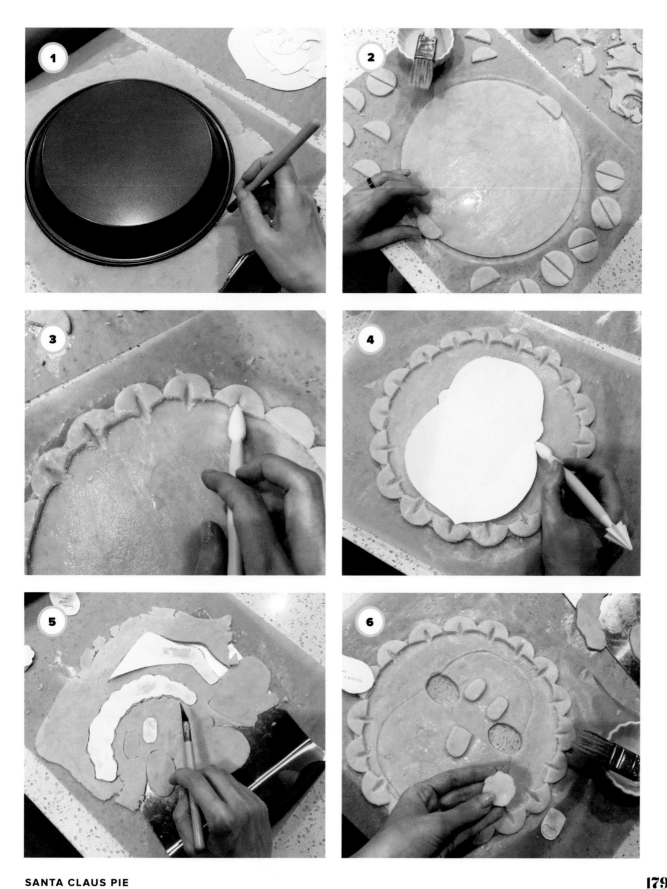

SANTA CLAUS PIE

(continued from page 178)

7. Paste down the strip of dough for Santa's hat trim with pasteurized egg whites, and using your fingernails, "squinch" up the dough to create a fur-like texture on the hat trim and pom-pom.

8. Paste Santa's mittens down with pasteurized egg whites, then, using the fondant sculpting tool, score some vertical lines along the cuffs and small horizontal lines everywhere else to mimic the "stitches" of a knitted texture.

9. Use a food-safe artist brush to give the pie a vanilla wash with a mixture of vanilla extract and a tiny bit of the brown gel food color everywhere except Santa's skin areas.

10. Mix the gel food colors with vanilla extract. (Add 1½ teaspoons of vanilla extract to a ramekin, then dab a generous toothpick full of gel color on the edge of the ramekin. Dip your food-safe artist brush into the vanilla and then into the pigment on the side and paint away!) Paint the mittens, hat, and tongue with the red gel food color. Paint Santa's nose with the pink gel food color (adding a white shine mark with the white icing color if you want) and the hat trim with the white icing color. (Remember, Santa's nose is not yet attached and will be baked separately!) Finally, paint Santa's eyes with the black gel food color, adding white shine marks with the white icing color.

11. Carefully place the parchment paper with your top decoration onto the baking sheet and bake at 400°F (200°C; gas mark 6) for 14 minutes, or

Pie-Modding Ideas

You can use meringue to enhance pie designs in a number of different ways. Try using it to create a snowy meadow, a snowman, or a person's hairdo. And adding gel food colors to meringue opens up even more options for decoration, like palette-knife flower painting (Google it; it's so pretty!) or abstract scenes.

until golden brown. Bake Santa's nose separately, taking it out after 8 minutes. While your top decoration and nose cool, bake your base pie with an infinity edge. As soon as your base pie comes out of the oven, bubbling hot, carefully place your Santa on top with the cake lifter. Lightly press down for 10 seconds so that the top and base fuse together. Let the pie cool for a bit, and then pipe on the first layer of meringue for Santa's beard. Do not add his moustache yet.

12. Torch the beard layer of meringue with the kitchen torch. Pipe on meringue for Santa's moustache, then place his nose on top of the moustache. Sprinkle the pink sanding sugar through the holes for his cheeks. Use the hashtags #SantaPie and #PiesAreAwesomeTheBook when you post pics of your version of this pie—I'd love to see what you create!

Clock Pie

It's five minutes to midnight, so get your noisemakers ready! Okay, this clock actually says it's five minutes to one o'clock in the morning, but who's counting? It's a party! And what better way to be crowned queen of that party than to show up with this scrumptious baroque clock pie for your hosts?

Level: Intermediate

Ingredients

+ Dough of your choice for 1 double-crust pie
+ Pasteurized egg white (or almond milk if making a vegan pie)
+ Vanilla extract
+ Brown gel food color
+ Gold sugar pearls or dragées (optional)
+ Sugar glue (such as Wilton Dab-N-Hold Edible Adhesive) (optional)

Supplies

+ Parchment paper
+ Rolling pin
+ Food-safe precision blade
+ Ramekins or small containers to hold pasteurized egg whites and mix vanilla wash
+ Pastry brush
+ Fondant sculpting tool (or toothpick)
+ Food-safe artist brush
+ Flower-shaped cookie cutters or plunger cutters (optional)
+ Baking sheets
+ Pie pan of your choice
+ Cake lifter

Dough of Your Choice
This is one of the more fiddly pies in the book, so you may want to stay away from all-butter doughs for this one. All-shortening, store-bought, or cookie-style dough will give you the sharpest details.

Base Pie
Create an infinity-edge base pie with the filling extending all the way to the edges (see page 60). Use any type of filling, but your composition will pop the best if you choose a dark filling that contrasts with the color of the baked dough.

Resources
For instructions on downloading and printing the template for this pie, go to page 206.

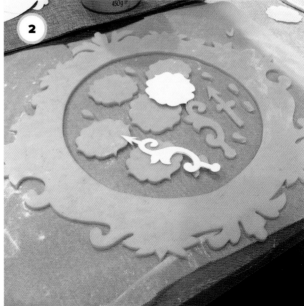

1. Roll out your dough on a piece of parchment paper with your rolling pin. Place your templates on the rolled-out dough and cut out the shapes with your food-safe precision blade. Remove the templates.

2. Because the trim template is larger than a standard sheet of paper, only half of it appears on the template sheet for this project. After you have cut out one side of your pie frame, you will need to flip the template over to cut out the other side, which will be a mirror image of the side you just cut.

✦ Jessica's Tip ✦

If you would like to add a second hand to your clock, use a stainless-steel ruler to cut a very thin strip of dough. Bake it at 400°F (200°C; gas mark 6) for 4 minutes by itself on a baking sheet. Make a few of them in case you break them when transferring them to the pie!

3. Glue the four small medallions to the clock frame with pasteurized egg whites and the pastry brush, and then give the entire design a generous coating of pasteurized egg whites.

4. Using the fondant sculpting tool, score decorative lines around the clock frame and Roman numerals into the medallion panels. You can emulate my designs or create your own design comprised of dots, dashed lines, and/or swirls.

5. Use the food-safe artist brush to give the entire clock a vanilla wash with a mixture of vanilla extract and a tiny bit of brown gel food color, making sure the mixture seeps into all the cracks.

6. Now it is time to make the decorative flower shapes! If you have flower-shaped cutters, save yourself a lot of time and use those to cut out the flower shapes; otherwise, use the provided templates. Use the fondant sculpting tool to score the middle detail lines on the flowers, and then give them a vanilla wash. Carefully place the parchment paper with your clock and flowers on separate baking sheets and bake at 400°F (200°C; gas mark 6) for 12 minutes, or until golden brown. While the pieces are cooling, make your base pie with an infinity edge. As soon as your base pie comes out of the oven, bubbling hot, carefully place your clock on top with the cake lifter. Add the flowers with a dab of pie filling or some sugar glue. Finish your pie off with some gold sugar pearls placed around the perimeter. Use the hashtags #ClockPie and #PiesAreAwesomeTheBook when you post pics of your version of this pie—I'd love to see what you create!

Pie-Modding Ideas

There are many options for pretty pie designs within this frame! You can use the clock's frame without the Roman numeral panels as a nice trim design for all sorts of pies. Try adding words inside the frame, such as a scrolly "Give Thanks" for Thanksgiving. You could also trace a loved one's profile on a piece of paper and add a dough version of that to the center of your frame. Or arrange a series of tiny cutout flowers in a grid to emulate a pretty wallpaper pattern.

Flying Unicorn Pie

Nothing says "Happy Birthday!" better than a unicorn pie . . . unless, maybe, it's a flying unicorn pie on a rainbow sprinkle background! This pie consists of some simple cutout dough pieces pasted together and baked separately before being added to the finished baked pie. My favorite thing about this joyful design is that you can tweak it to match your own party colors. You're guaranteed to get a delightful squeal out of whomever you place this pie in front of! Unless they hate unicorns . . . in which case, you probably shouldn't be friends with them anyway. Just sayin'.

Level: Beginner

Ingredients

- ✦ Dough of your choice for 1 double-crust pie
- ✦ Pasteurized egg whites (or almond milk if making a vegan pie)
- ✦ Vanilla extract
- ✦ Brown gel food color
- ✦ Gel food colors of your choice (optional)
- ✦ Assortment of sanding sugar, sprinkles, and sugar pearls or dragées
- ✦ Edible adhesive (such as jam, chocolate, sugar glue, or leftover filling)
- ✦ Gold and pearl luster dusts
- ✦ Vodka (or any clear alcohol or extract to mix with the luster dusts)

Supplies

- ✦ Parchment paper
- ✦ Rolling pin
- ✦ Paper templates
- ✦ Food-safe precision blade
- ✦ Ramekins or small containers to hold pasteurized egg whites and mix color
- ✦ Pastry brush
- ✦ Fondant sculpting tool (or toothpick)
- ✦ Food-safe artist brushes
- ✦ Baking sheet
- ✦ Pie pan of your choice
- ✦ Metal spatula

Dough of Your Choice

You can use cookie-style, gluten-free, rough puff, all-butter, or vegan dough interchangeably.

Base Pie

Create a base pie with a decorative crimped edge. Because this pie top is fully covered with sanding sugar, you can use any flavor of filling you like. I made an apple pie with a standard shortcrust.

★ Jessica's Tip ★

Since you are going to be coating the top of this pie in sanding sugar, select a filling that is not overly sweet—maybe even pick something tart—and don't put any sugar in your crust. Unless you have a reeeeal sweet tooth. In which case, go nuts!

Resources

For instructions on downloading and printing the template for this pie, go to page 206. For edge-crimping suggestions, see page 60.

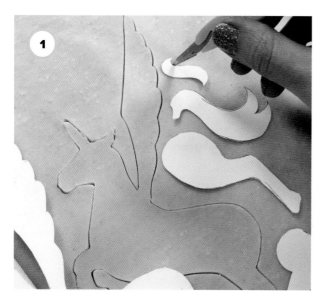

1. Roll out your dough ⅛ inch (3 mm) thick on a piece of parchment paper with your rolling pin. Place your templates and cut out all the shapes with your food-safe precision blade. Cut out as many "rays" as you like. I cut out eight. Don't worry if they look long; they'll shrink in the oven!

2. Coat all the pieces in pasteurized egg whites with the pastry brush, then paste the unicorn pieces together. Smooth out the joins with the back of your fingernail or the fondant sculpting tool. If you have any trouble lifting the pieces, just pop them in the freezer for 2 minutes, then use a spatula to lift them.

3. Score some details in the unicorn's wings, tail, mane, and face with the fondant sculpting tool.

4. Use a food-safe artist brush to give your unicorn a quick vanilla wash with a mixture of vanilla extract and a tiny bit of brown gel food color, making sure the mixture seeps into the cracks. (Instead of using a vanilla wash, you can paint the unicorn with gel food colors at this point. Just make sure you choose colors that will stand out from your background!) Carefully place the parchment paper with your pieces onto a baking sheet and bake your unicorn and rays at 400°F (200°C; gas mark 6) for 8 to 10 minutes, or until golden brown.

5. While the unicorn and ray pieces cool, make your base pie with a crimped edge. As soon as your base pie comes out of the oven, bubbling hot, carefully place your cooled ray pieces evenly around the top with the spatula.

6. Let the pie completely cool, and then add the edible bling of your choice (this is the fun part!). I chose a rainbow assortment of sanding sugar and sugar pearls. Finally, place a dab of the edible adhesive in the center and place your unicorn with the spatula. Now you can add the luster dusts mixed with a few drops of vodka for a bit more fabulousness. Let's face it, we can all use a bit more fabulousness. Use the hashtags #FlyingUnicornPie and #PiesAreAwesomeTheBook when you post pics of your version of this pie—I'd love to see what you create!

Pie-Modding Ideas

There are many alternate designs that will work with this technique—any large central image on a background of colorful rays will look awesome. Try cookie-cutter shapes paired with different color schemes for different occasions. Maybe red and blue stripes with a big star in the middle for the Fourth of July, or black and gold rays for New Year's Eve, or red and green with a Santa head for Christmas! Or something with dinosaurs! Or . . . well, you tell me! I know you'll come up with something fabulous!

PieKabobs

Nothing is more awkward than being served a delicious plated dish at a party when there is no place to sit! Sadly, most traditional pies fall into that "hard to walk around with" category. Does that mean that pies don't get an invite to the party? No way! Introducing my latest creation: PieKabobs—tiny, delicious pies on a sturdy skewer, dressed to impress. Serve these either standing or fanned out on your dessert buffet table. You won't need three guesses to figure out which treat your guests will be making a beeline for!

Level: Beginner

Ingredients

+ Dough of your choice for 1 double-crust pie, plus more if needed (depending on how many you want to make)
+ Maraschino cherries
+ 3 colors of candy melts or melting chocolate wafers
+ Assortment of small sprinkles, sanding sugar, and crushed nuts, for topping

Supplies

+ 24-cup mini muffin pan
+ 2½- to 3-inch (6 to 7.5 cm) round cookie cutter, measuring cup, or glass
+ Parchment paper
+ Large piping bag
+ Very sharp knife
+ Candy melter or small microwave-safe bowls
+ 8-inch (20 cm) lollipop sticks

Dough of Your Choice

I used the Sweet Pie Dough on page 216 for this project, as it is sturdy enough to stay on the lollipop sticks even under the most vigorous child manhandling. If you are serving adults, any dough will do.

Base Pie

All you need is 24-cup mini muffin pan and your favorite filling to make these tiny pies! I used my Banana Cream Cheese Icebox Pie Filling on page 225.

 Jessica's Tip

Have no time to make your own dough for this project? No problem! Just pick up some prefab mini tart shells from the store and off you go!

1. Roll out your dough ¼ inch (6 mm) thick on a piece of parchment paper with your rolling pin. This dough is rolled out slightly thicker than the usual ⅛ inch (3 mm) to help the shells hold up when you cut the holes into the piecrusts for the lollipop sticks in step 5. Cut out twenty-four circles with the round cookie cutter.

2. Line each muffin cup with a small strip of parchment paper that extends beyond the cup to make it easy to pop the shells out after baking. Press your dough circles into the cups with your fingers or using whatever you have on hand as a tamper. Bake at 400°F (200°C; gas mark 6) for 10 minutes, or until done.

3. Remove the shells from the pan and set them aside to cool. Transfer your filling of choice to a large piping bag.

4. Pipe the filling into your cooled tart shells and let set in the refrigerator for 2 hours (or for however long your filling requires).

5. Using the very sharp knife, cut two holes on opposite sides of the crust of each mini pie for the lollipop sticks. Do not press the knife into the crust; instead, slowly twist it in a circle to create the hole. Make the holes just large enough to fit the diameter of a lollipop stick.

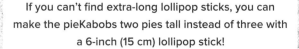

6. Cut a similar hole in the bottom of each of the maraschino cherries, then feed the lollipop sticks through three of the mini pies, leaving just enough of the stick protruding from the top for the cherry to fit.

7. Melt your three colors of candy melts in the candy melter or microwave according to the package directions, then add the melted chocolates to piping bags or resealable plastic bags with a corner cut off. Pipe the chocolate on top of the mini pies, making sure to overlap the pies a little bit. This helps them fuse together and stay on the stick.

8. Before the chocolate sets, quickly sprinkle on your toppings. Now chill your PieKabobs in the fridge for at least 2 hours (or even overnight), then serve. Use the hashtags #PieKabobs and #PiesAreAwesomeTheBook when you post pics of your version of this pie—I'd love to see what you create!

Pie-Modding Ideas

While I really love the playful banana-split look of this pie, if you are looking for a more sophisticated option, you can string three tiny pies of complementary flavors on your sticks, topped with a classic lattice design, a solid top, or even letters to spell out a short message made from pie dough—"I <3 U" or a wedding couple's initials with an "&" in the middle perhaps?

Mama and Baby Bear Pies

Gender-reveal parties are so 2019 . . . What are you having? A cute baby, that's what! So why not cater your baby shower gathering with some equally cute treats? This mama and baby bear pie set can be easily customized to jive with your color scheme and party decor by changing up the items the bears are holding. If you are feeling ambitious, you can even create a full set of tart-size bears for your guests, or, better yet, make them together as one of your party activities!

Level: Beginner

Ingredients

✦ Dough of your choice for 2 double-crust pies

✦ Pasteurized egg whites (or almond milk if making a vegan pie)

✦ Gel food colors of your choice

✦ Vanilla extract

✦ Opaque white icing color (optional)

Supplies

✦ Parchment paper

✦ Rolling pin

✦ Paper templates

✦ Food-safe precision blade

✦ Heart- and flag-shaped cutters (optional)

✦ Ramekins or small containers to hold pasteurized egg whites and mix color

✦ Pastry brush

✦ Fondant sculpting tool (or toothpick)

✦ Toothpicks (for the gel food colors)

✦ Food-safe artist brushes

✦ Baking sheets

✦ 2 pie or tart pans of different sizes

✦ Cake lifter

Dough of Your Choice

Any dough will work with this simple design!

Base Pie

Create two base pies, one large and one small. If using pie pans, create pies with an infinity edge (see page 60). Select a filling that will contrast with the color of your bears. I used my Banana Cream Cheese Icebox Pie Filling on page 225 but flavored it with honey instead of banana.

 Jessica's Tip

Resize the paper templates to fit whatever size pie or tart pans you have on hand.

Resources

For instructions on downloading and printing the template for this pie, go to page 206.

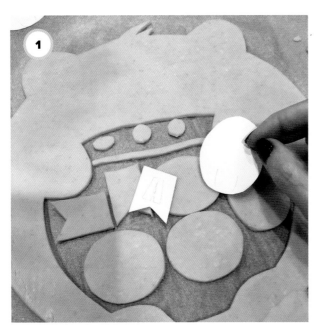

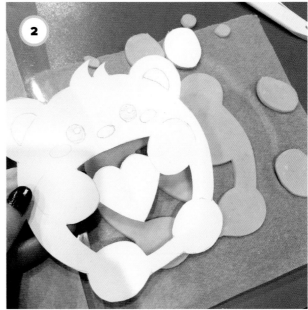

1. Roll out your dough ⅛ inch (3 mm) thick on a piece of parchment paper with your rolling pin. Place the paper templates for the mama bear on the rolled-out dough and cut out all the shapes with your food-safe precision blade. Remove the templates.

2. Place the paper templates for the baby bear on the rolled-out dough and cut out all the shapes. Remove the templates. (If you have heart- and flag-shaped cutters on hand, you can use those in place of the templates.)

✷ Jessica's Tip ✷

If you have other cutter shapes on hand, you can opt to have the bears hold something different, like a rubber ducky, flower, or even the baby's name.

3. Coat the dough pieces in pasteurized egg whites with the pastry brush, then paste the pieces together. Using the fondant sculpting tool, score the details for the ears and paws.

4. Paint your bears using gel food colors mixed with vanilla extract. (Add 1½ teaspoons of vanilla extract to a ramekin, then dab a generous toothpick full of gel color on the edge of the ramekin. Dip your food-safe artist brush into the vanilla and then into the pigment on the side and paint away!) I opted to keep the bodies of the bears unpainted, but feel free to paint them white, pink, brown, or whatever color you fancy!

5. Carefully place the parchment paper with the bears onto the baking sheets and bake at 400°F (200°C; gas mark 6) for 12 minutes. Let them completely cool.

6. While the bears are cooling, bake your base pie. If using a filling similar to mine, you will need to blind-bake the shells before adding the filling (see page 226 and the Resources section on page 228 for instructions on how to blind-bake pie shells). Make the pie filling, pipe or spoon it into the cooled blind-baked shells, and let the base pies set in the refrigerator for 2 hours. When your base pies are set, carefully place the bears on top with the cake lifter. (If using a cooked filling, place the bears on top when the pies come bubbling hot out of the oven.) You may then paint on smaller details, like white shine on the eyes or fine lines for their smiles. Use the hashtags #BabyShowerPie and #PiesAreAwesomeTheBook when you post pics of your version of this pie—I'd love to see what you create!

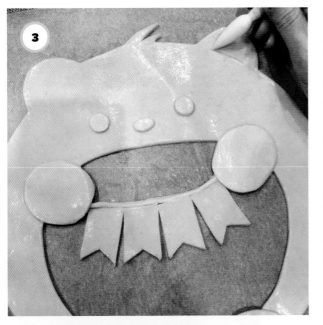

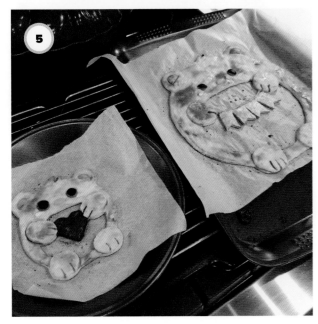

Pie-Modding Ideas

Not into bears? How about bunnies, doggies, or piggies? With a few quick tweaks to the ear and nose shapes, you'll have a whole new set of chonky animals to delight your guests. Or try a whole barnyard full of different animals!

Piescraper

Congrats on your big day! A day for big dresses, big receptions, and big pies! One of the reasons pies have taken a back seat to cake at weddings is the fact that the "main wedding dessert" is as much a part of the decor as it is the catering. That all-important side profile determines the size of the "wow!" uttered by guests as they enter the venue and see the dessert for the first time. Even people who adore pies and have no time for cake usually feel compelled to purchase the ubiquitous multitier wedding cake, as that is "just how it's done." Well, not anymore! Meet the Piescraper—the challenger to cake's claim on wedding-dessert supremacy. This tutorial is for a two-tier Piescraper with top ornamentation, but I have made perfectly sturdy three-tier Piescrapers in the past as well. Just remember to assemble it in place at the venue to avoid a white-knuckle car ride over!

Level: Advanced

Ingredients

+ Dough of your choice for 2 double-crust pies, plus extra if making tarts
+ Wafer paper
+ Pink icing color (optional)
+ Opaque white icing color
+ Pasteurized egg whites (or almond milk if making a vegan pie)
+ Gel food colors of your choice
+ Vanilla extract
+ Brown gel food color
+ Clear sanding sugar
+ ½ cup (85 g) white candy melts or melting chocolate wafers

Supplies

+ 2 deep-dish tart pans of different sizes
+ Rolling pin
+ 6-inch (15 cm) stainless-steel spool
+ Dessert stand
+ Paper templates
+ Scissors
+ Food-safe artist brushes
+ Parchment paper
+ Food-safe precision blade
+ Silicone border molds (optional)
+ Ramekins or small containers to hold pasteurized egg whites and mix color

+ Pastry brush
+ Fondant sculpting tool (or toothpick)
+ Stainless-steel ruler (optional)
+ Baking sheets
+ Large piping bags
+ Toothpicks (for the gel food colors)
+ Candy melter or small microwave-safe bowls
+ Small piping bags or resealable plastic bags
+ Food-safe freeze spray (optional)
+ Medium piping bag with a decorative tip
+ Metal spatula

Dough of Your Choice
For this design, select a dough that can stand up on its own outside of the pan, such as the Sweet Pie Dough on page 216.

Base Pie
Create two deep-dish tarts of different sizes. Prepare a filling that can be piped or poured into the shells—mousses, custards, or chiffons are all good options. For this particular pie, I used two different layers of filling: a strawberry cream cheese mousse and a denser top layer of strawberry custard.

Resources
For instructions on downloading and printing the template for this pie, go to page 206. For edge-crimping suggestions, see page 60.

1. Begin by doing a test setup of your armature. Place your tart pans and stainless-steel spool on top of your dessert stand and hold the paper template of the topper in place to check if you are happy with the height. If all looks good, measure the height of the spool and the heights of the sides of the tart pans. Make note of these numbers and adjust the paper stencils meant to cover the spool to the correct size for your pie. My spool is 6 inches (15 cm), and the existing template is set up for that size. When you're ready to make your Piescraper, set out the dough and all the supplies you will need for this project so that once you start working, everything is at hand. (In the photos, you will see that I also made a mini tart to sit alongside the Piescraper. These instructions only focus on the Piescraper, but you are welcome to also make a mini tart!)

⋆ Jessica's Tip ⋆

Remember, different types of dough will shrink different amounts, so bake a test panel and measure it against your spool before you go ahead and make all the finished decorated pieces!

---

2. Roll out your dough for the base pies and line your two tart pans. You will need to blind-bake the shells before adding the filling (see page 226 and the Resources section on page 228 for instructions on how to blind-bake pie shells). Feel free to make these the day before if you would like to spread out the work. Just store the baked shells in a cool, dry place.

3. Using the butterfly wing templates as guides, cut out about ten sets of wings from wafer paper with clean scissors. If desired, paint the wings pink and white with opaque icing color to match the photo or feel free to leave them white, which looks pretty too! Set them somewhere out of the way to dry for several hours.

4. Roll out some more dough 1/8 inch (3 mm) thick on pieces of parchment paper (this will likely fill up two or three different sheets of parchment, as it is a big pie!) for the decorative pieces and the two triangular support props for the topper. Place the paper templates on the rolled-out dough and cut out the shapes with your food-safe precision blade. Cut out enough of the medallions that will go around the sides of the tarts—at least six of the smaller ones for the top and eight of the larger ones for the bottom.

5. If you have silicone border molds handy, create some trim decoration to line your topper. Paste the trim onto your topper piece with pasteurized egg whites. If you don't have a border mold, you can use your fondant sculpting tool to score decorative lines instead.

6. Coat all your pieces in pasteurized egg whites with the pastry brush to keep them from drying out. Add some additional decorations to your pieces if you would like to spiff up the detail and give them more of a "brooch" aesthetic. To accomplish this, you can cut small strips of dough and coil them around the panels like a ribbon, or roll some little balls of dough and paste these on with pasteurized egg whites to emulate pearls, or you could add cutout leaf or flower shapes—whatever looks pretty to you!

(continued on page 203)

(continued from page 200)

7. You can easily add additional decorative interest by poking little holes with your fondant sculpting tool. This gives the shapes a jewelry-like quality. Feel free to make the details your own! Use whatever tools you have on hand.

8. Paint the insides of the topper and the little medallions with the white icing color. Use a food-safe artist brush to give everything else a vanilla wash with a mixture of vanilla extract and a tiny bit of brown gel food color, making sure the mixture seeps into all the cracks.

9. Carefully place the parchment paper with your decorative pieces onto baking sheets and bake at 350°F (175°C; gas mark 4) for 6 to 10 minutes, making sure to remove the small pieces at the 6-minute mark. (As you can see in the photo, I forgot to do that. Oops!)

10. Now you are ready to create the panels that will cover the spool. Cut out approximately four each of the thick and thin panels in place on a piece of parchment paper. Don't try to lift them up from the paper! They should bake right where you cut them.

11. Paint a larger panel, which will be facing the front, with the white icing color. Feel free to add some decorative trim to the panels, either with a border mold or by gently scoring lines with a stainless-steel ruler. Give all the pieces a vanilla wash, and then bake at 350°F (175°C; gas mark 4) for 8 minutes.

12. Let all the components for your Piescraper completely cool before you start to assemble. You can leave them someplace cool and dry overnight (that is, if you don't have an adventurous cat roaming the house!). Use this time to make your pie fillings, transfer them to large piping bags, and place them in the fridge. Once your pieces have cooled, you can paint some flowers onto the white areas using your gel food colors mixed with vanilla extract. (Add 1½ teaspoons of vanilla extract to a ramekin, then dab a generous toothpick full of gel food color on the edge of the ramekin. Dip your food-safe artist brush into the vanilla and then into the pigment on the side and paint away!) Start with very light lines (more vanilla than color), and then build them up when you are happy with the look. For the final coat, use straight pigment to darken the main lines and parts of the flowers you would like to highlight.

(continued on page 204)

(continued from page 203)

13. Now we are ready to assemble our Piescraper! All of the steps from here should take place at the venue, in the spot where the pie will be displayed. Melt your candy melts in your candy melter and set it to "keep warm." If you don't have a candy melter, melt your candy melts in a microwave-safe bowl according to the package directions. Transfer a small amount of melted chocolate to a small piping bag or resealable plastic bag with the corner snipped off and pipe small lines on a sheet of parchment paper for the butterfly bodies for your wafer-paper wings. Use the food-safe freeze spray to instantly lock the wings in place on the bodies or find some small objects to hold the wings up while they set. This should take about 2 minutes to set up and stay in place without the freeze spray.

14. Now it's time to focus on the tart shells. Set out your dessert stand and place a dot of melted chocolate down to hold the larger bottom shell in place. Add some melted chocolate to a medium piping bag with a decorative tip. I used a star tip for this project. Pipe a row of chocolate roses around the rim of the tart shell. Attach the medallions to the outsides of the shells with dots of melted chocolate and hold them in place until they set or use the freeze spray to lock them in place. Pipe a ring of melted chocolate in the center of the tart shell and gently affix the (clean) stainless-steel spool.

15. Now add the panels around the spool with the melted chocolate to cover it. Pipe a line of chocolate where you will be placing your front-facing panel on the bottom of your tart shell. Once the panel is in place, pipe a line of chocolate along the top of it to help it adhere to the spool. Hold it in place until the chocolate sets. This will take about 2 minutes (unless you have some food-safe freeze spray, then it will take less than 2 seconds!). Continue placing the rest of the panels around the spool in this fashion. When they are all in place, seal them together by piping a final line of chocolate along the seams where they meet.

★ Jessica's Tip ★

If you are finding it challenging to cover the support spool with dough ornamentation, consider going with a more decorative prop and leaving it exposed. There are a number of options available in cake decorating shops and online that you can try out. Lucite cylinders, little white fluted pillars, small tree stumps, mirrored cylinders . . . you can get very creative with your supports!

16. Glue the bottom metal circle from your smaller tart pan on top of the spool and panels with melted chocolate, then glue the second shell on top of that. This provides some extra stability for the top layer. Use the food-grade freeze spray to speed up the setting time; otherwise, wait at least 2 minutes before moving on to the next step.

17. Glue in place the pie topper and its support prop. Using the freeze spray and a dot of melted chocolate, attach the butterflies anywhere you think looks pretty! If you don't have freeze spray hold them in place for 2 minutes until they set.

18. Remove the pie fillings from the fridge and pipe in your layers. You can hit it with a bit of freeze spray from at least a foot away if you feel it needs to set up a bit more—just don't spray too closely or you'll blast your filling all over the place! Now you are ready to let the guests in and blow their minds with your fabulous wedding Piescraper. Use the hashtags #Piescraper and #PiesAreAwesomeTheBook when you post pics of your version of this pie—I'd love to see what you create!

Pie-Modding Ideas

You can personalize the topper with the wedding couple's initials by first tracing a decorative font from your computer to make a template, and then cutting the shapes out of dough and adding them to the medallion. Or you could create a pastry version of the couple's favorite cartoon characters, flowers, birds, dragons . . . anything goes!

Templates

Detailed step-by-step instructions on how to save, open, resize, print, and trace off the screen are provided at the link!

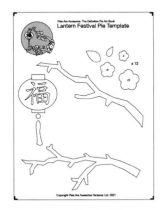

Lantern Festival Pie
LUNAR NEW YEAR

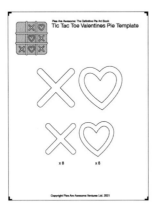

Tic-Tac-Toe Pie
VALENTINE'S DAY

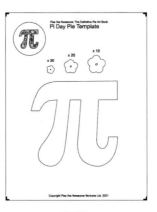

Pi Pie
PI DAY

Leprechaun Hat Pie
ST. PATRICK'S DAY

Bunny Pie (1)
EASTER

Bunny Pie (2)
EASTER

Folk Art Bee Pie
EARTH DAY

You can download the full-size versions of all the templates at this link:
https://www.piesareawesome.com/pages/resources

You can download the full-size versions of all the templates at this link:
https://www.piesareawesome.com/pages/resources

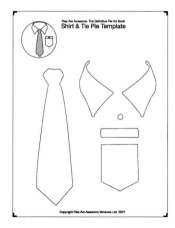

Shirt and Tie Pie
FATHER'S DAY

Stars and Stripes Pie
FOURTH OF JULY

Paris Skyline Pie (1)
BASTILLE DAY

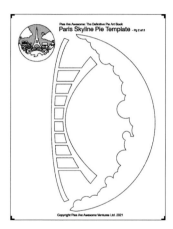

Paris Skyline Pie (2)
BASTILLE DAY

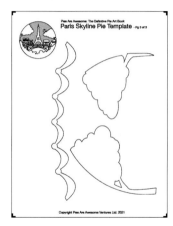

Paris Skyline Pie (3)
BASTILLE DAY

Mandala Pie (1)
DIWALI

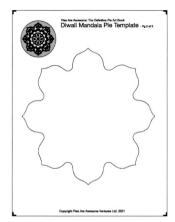

Mandala Pie (2)
DIWALI

Mandala Pie (3)
DIWALI

Chibi Pumpkin Pie
HALLOWEEN

You can download the full-size versions of all the templates at this link:
https://www.piesareawesome.com/pages/resources

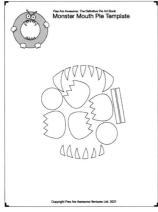

Monster Mouth Pie

HALLOWEEN

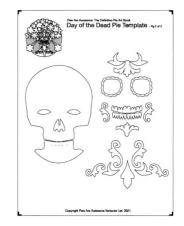

La Catrina Pie (1)

DAY OF THE DEAD

La Catrina Pie (2)

DAY OF THE DEAD

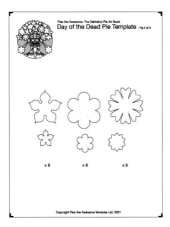

La Catrina Pie (3)

DAY OF THE DEAD

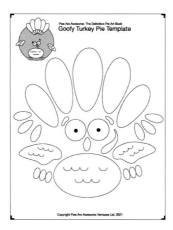

Goofy Turkey Pie

THANKSGIVING

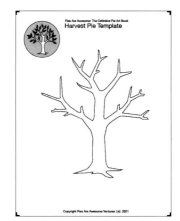

Harvest Tree Pie

THANKSGIVING

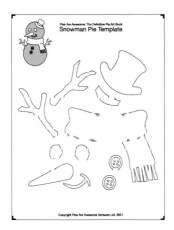

Snowman Pie

WINTER HOLIDAYS

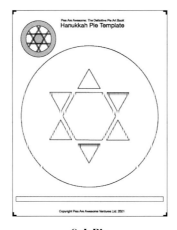

Gelt Pie

HANUKKAH

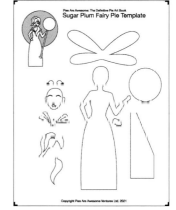

Sugar Plum Fairy Pie Doll

CHRISTMAS

You can download the full-size versions of all the templates at this link:
https://www.piesareawesome.com/pages/resources

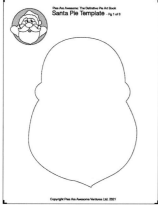

Santa Claus Pie (1)
CHRISTMAS

Santa Claus Pie (2)
CHRISTMAS

Santa Claus Pie (3)
CHRISTMAS

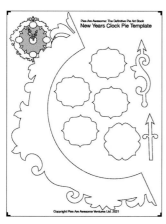

Clock Pie
NEW YEAR'S EVE

Flying Unicorn Pie
BIRTHDAY

Mama and Baby Bear Pies (1)
BABY SHOWER

Mama and Baby Bear Pies (2)
BABY SHOWER

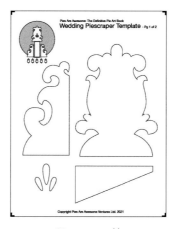

Piescraper (1)
WEDDING

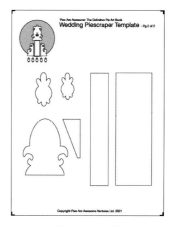

Piescraper (2)
WEDDING

Pie Dough and Filling Recipes

While this book is primarily a Pie Art "technique" book, and the projects are intended to work with your own tried-and-true dough and filling recipes, I wanted to make sure you still had access to some recipes to get you started, in case you don't already have your own collection.

Pie Dough Recipes

In the following pages, you will find six pie dough recipes—three of my own and three created by good friends of mine who are exceptionally talented bakers! These recipes are some of my favorites for their dietary versatility, flavor, texture, and pliability in working with Pie Art designs. But don't feel constrained to only use these recipes for your projects! You are more than welcome to work with Grandma's secret all-butter recipe, the recipe on the back of the Crisco box, or your favorite brand of store-bought roll-out dough. Just be sure to conduct ThePieous's Dough Test (see page 23) with each new dough before you embark upon a full Pie Art project. And if you are looking for more inspiration, I have included links to a number of excellent pie dough recipes online in the Resources section on page 228, where you'll find recipes for chocolate pie dough, classic all-butter doughs, rough puff pastry, and more.

As with all recipes that rely on chemical reactions, your mileage may vary with these, and any, pie dough recipes—where you live in the world, the time of year, the weather, the brand of ingredients you use, the technique you use to measure ingredients, the age and make of your oven, and a host of other small variables can have big impacts on pie dough. I live in the Pacific Northwest, use a gas oven, and measure ingredients by weight rather than volume. What is just right for me may be super sticky if you live in a humid region or super dry if you live at a high altitude. Your bake time may be several minutes longer or shorter depending on the kind of oven you are using and whether it has any "hot spots." The amount of flour you end up with in your dough may be way more or less than mine depending on how lightly or densely you pack it into a measuring cup (this is why I always use a kitchen scale to weigh it). The amount of liquid you need in your recipe may change depending on the brand of butter you are using and its native water content.

And all of this is okay! After you've tried making one of these recipes once, and have conducted

your dough test, you'll know whether you need to tweak the amount of flour or water or fat or the bake time to suit your environment best. Just refer to the Troubleshooting section on page 71 for instructions on how to make your adjustments, and you'll be on your way. There may be no such thing as a "fool-proof" pie dough recipe, but we aim to get as close to "fool-resistant" as we can!

Pie Filling Recipes

The six pie dough recipes (along with any store-bought dough) can be paired with pretty much any filling—even canned pie filling if you are in a hurry! But in the interest of ensuring that this book remains a "one-stop shop" for pie bakers who may not have a plethora of favorite pie filing recipes at the ready, I have included a few of mine.

Half-Butter/ Half-Shortening Shortcrust

This recipe is my "Goldilocks" recipe—it's pretty flaky, tastes pretty good, is pretty easy to work with, and is pretty easy to make. Other recipes may have it beat in one of those categories—puff pastry is the flakiest, all-butter shortcrust tastes the best (to me), store-bought dough is the easiest to work with, etc.—but I haven't found any other dough that comes as close to being "just right" in every category as this one! If you're looking for one pie dough recipe to try out first, this is your boy.

Yield: 1 double-crust pie

Ingredients

+ 150 grams (¾ cup) cold shortening
+ 150 grams (⅔ cup) cold unsalted European-style butter*
+ 525 grams (4 cups) all-purpose flour, divided
+ 2 tablespoons sugar
+ 1 teaspoon salt
+ 6 tablespoons cold water

If you don't have "Euro butter," you may need to add a little less water at the end because North American–style butter naturally has more water.

1. About an hour before you want to make your dough, place a large metal mixing bowl in the fridge to chill it. When you are ready to start, get out all your ingredients and supplies, and set out three pieces of plastic wrap (if you have the room) on the counter. This is where you will wrap up your balls of dough later, and it's nice to have them ready to go so that you aren't fumbling around with the plastic wrap box with your cruddy dough hands.

2. Place a plate or bowl onto a food scale and tare the scale (set it to zero). Measure out the shortening and butter on the scale (they can be in the same bowl, as long as the weight adds up to 300 grams). Cut the shortening and butter into roughly 1-inch (2.5 cm) pats and stick them in the fridge to wait their turn.

3. Now place a clean bowl on the scale, tare it, and measure out 250 grams (2 cups) of the flour. Add the flour to a food processor. Add the sugar and salt to the flour and pulse it four or five times. If you don't have a food processor, simply mix the ingredients by hand. Just make sure your hands and any tools you use are cold!

4. Take the shortening and butter out of the fridge and evenly spread the pats around the flour in the mixer. Try to alternate pats of butter and pats of shortening if you can.

5. Pulse the mixer between twenty-five and forty times until the mixture completely clumps together into a paste. Everyone's idea of a "pulse" is different, so it may take you more or less pulses—just refer to the image to know when you're there!

6. With a rubber spatula, spread the mixture around so that it evenly coats the bottom of the mixer again.

7. Measure out 200 grams (1½ cups) of the flour in your bowl on the scale. Evenly sprinkle this flour around the paste in the mixer and pulse five times.

⭐ Jessica's Tip ⭐

Because you are creating a paste out of your fat and half of your flour rather than taking pains to not fully incorporate the fat, it's really hard to overwork this dough—thanks to the brilliant J. Kenji López-Alt for pie-oneering the "paste method" of dough mixing!—and you'll still get great flaky layers at the end. It may seem a bit odd if you are used to the "you must retain pea-size chunks of frozen fat or else!" way of making pie dough, but try it out and see what you think! It certainly removes a lot of the stress of the ticking clock, and you don't have to panic quite so much about keeping everything cold, cold, cold.

8. Now get the cold metal bowl out of the fridge and dump the mixture from the food processor into the bowl. Watch out for the blade! Quickly "fluff up" the mixture with your hands, breaking the big chunks up into roughly 1-inch (2.5 cm) pieces. Sprinkle the cold water evenly around the dough, then sprinkle between 50 and 75 (6 and 8 tablespoons) of the remaining flour around the bowl. Start with 50 grams (6 tablespoons), and if the mixture is too sticky, add the last 25 grams (2 tablespoons). Use a fork to quickly incorporate the new flour and water into the existing paste chunks.

9. Follow the steps for Rolling Out Pie Dough on page 37 to wrap and prep your dough for the fridge, and you're done!

10. Bake time with this dough will vary depending on the filling recipe you choose to use, but plan for 400°F (200°C; gas mark 6) for around 50 minutes.

Vegan Pie Dough

The process for this Vegan Pie Dough recipe is more "traditional" than my Half-Butter/Half-Shortening Shortcrust recipe on page 212, so those of you who are pie-making veterans will feel right at home! This dough is one of my favorites not only because it is handy for times when I'm baking for vegan friends, but also because it doesn't puff up very much in the oven. It still has a great flavor from the almond milk and a nice flaky mouthfeel, but you don't have to worry about giant air bubbles or uneven warping in your carefully constructed Pie Art designs!

Yield: 1 double-crust pie

Ingredients

+ 350 grams (1⅔ cups) all-purpose flour
+ ½ teaspoon sugar
+ ½ teaspoon salt
+ ½ teaspoon xanthan gum (if you have it, makes the dough a bit more pliable and less prone to cracking when you handle it) (optional)
+ 200 grams (1 cup) cold Crisco or vegetable shortening of your choice
+ 4 tablespoons cold vanilla almond milk (or unsweetened for savory pies), plus 2 tablespoons as needed

1. About an hour before you want to make your dough, place a large metal mixing bowl in the fridge to chill it. When you are ready to start, get out all your ingredients and supplies, and set out three pieces of plastic wrap (if you have the room) on the counter. This is where you will wrap up your balls of dough later, and it's nice to have them ready to go so that you aren't fumbling around with the plastic wrap box with your cruddy dough hands.

2. Place a plate or bowl onto a food scale and tare the scale (set it to zero). Measure out the flour, sugar, salt, and xanthan gum (if using) and add to a food processor. Pulse the mixer a few times until fully combined. If you don't have a food processor, simply mix the ingredients by hand. Just make sure your hands and any tools you use are cold!

3. Measure out and cut the shortening into 1-inch (2.5 cm) pats. Add the pats to the food processor, evenly spreading them around the flour mixture.

4. Pulse the mixer eight to twelve times, or until your dough is crumbly with a few pea-size bits. Transfer the dough mixture to the cold metal mixing bowl.

5. Sprinkle 4 tablespoons of the cold almond milk evenly around the dough. Using a cold fork or your hands, "fluff up" the dough to incorporate the liquid. You will know it's done when you can "scrunch" a clump of dough and it stays together. If it falls apart after you let go, add up to 2 more tablespoons of cold almond milk. Oh! And if you happen to be somewhere really humid, and the 4 tablespoons of liquid made your dough too sticky, sprinkle a light dusting of flour on top—but no more than what you can pinch in your fingers!

6. Follow the steps for Rolling Out Pie Dough on page 37 to wrap and prep your dough for the fridge, and you're done!

7. Bake times with this dough will vary depending on the filling you choose to use, but a good starting place is 400°F (200°C; gas mark 6) for 50 minutes. Juicier fillings may require more time and initial heat, in which case you can try 425°F (220°C; gas mark 7) for 15 minutes, and then reduce the heat to 375°F (190°C; gas mark 5) for 45 minutes. You will know your pie is done when the filling (if it's a fruit filling) has been bubbling/boiling for 5 minutes.

✦ Jessica's Tip ✦

Feel free to get creative with different types of flavored almond milks for this recipe! (I'm partial to Silk brand's Vanilla Dairy-Free Soy Creamer.)

Sweet Pie Dough

This Sweet Pie Dough recipe—also referred to as a "cookie-style dough"—is the ultimate in terms of "structural integrity." It's not flaky like traditional shortcrust pastry, but it holds its shape perfectly, has a light, crisp flavor, and can stand on its own outside of the pie pan. It is a wonderful dough for making Piescrapers, Pie Dolls, free-standing tarts, Pietraits, or any type of Pie Art in which sturdiness and non-warping are benefits. It tastes like a mildly sweet shortbread cookie, and pairs well with pretty much any dessert filling.

Yield: 1 two-tier Piescraper plus 24 mini tarts

Ingredients

+ 500 grams (2¼ cups) unsalted European-style butter, softened
+ 400 grams (1¾ cups) caster sugar
+ ½ teaspoon salt
+ 4 egg yolks
+ 2 whole eggs
+ Lemon zest or 1 teaspoon vanilla or almond extract (optional)
+ 1000 grams (9¼ cups) pastry flour

1. Place a plate or bowl onto the food scale and tare the scale (set it to zero). Measure out the butter and set it out overnight to soften it. Unlike with shortcrust pastry recipes in which the fat needs to be super cold, for this recipe we will be creaming the butter.

2. When you are ready to start, get out all your ingredients and supplies, and set out three pieces of plastic wrap (if you have the room) on the counter. This is where you will wrap up your balls of dough later, and it's nice to have them ready to go so that you aren't fumbling around with the plastic-wrap box with your cruddy dough hands.

3. Measure out the sugar on the scale and place it in a large mixing bowl with the softened butter. Add the salt, and then cream everything together by hand or with a mixer until well combined and light and fluffy.

4. Add the egg yolks, whole eggs, and any flavoring (if using), and mix until smooth.

5. Measure out the pastry flour, then use a sifter to sift it into the bowl, adding roughly a third at a time, stirring to fully incorporate each time. Unlike with the shortcrust recipe on page 212, we really want to make sure our mixture is homogenous to avoid yucky flour lumps!

6. Follow the steps for Rolling Out Pie Dough on page 37 to wrap and prep your dough for the fridge, and you're done!

7. Cookie-like doughs, such as this one, don't require as high a temperature to bake as traditional shortcrust pastry. Try 350°F (175°C; gas mark 4) for about 20 to 30 minutes to blind-bake your tart shells, and when baking your dough with the filling already inside, defer to the instructions of the filling recipe.

 Jessica's Tip

The nice thing about this recipe is that it is very easy to halve, double, or even triple without having to worry about over- or undermixing. If you are making just one regular double-crust pie, feel free to freeze the rest for up to 3 months in a double freezer bag.

Courtney Ford's Gluten-Free Pie Dough

My friend Courtney Ford is not only an über-talented actor, but she also happens to be the best gluten-free baker I know! While she makes a mean gluten-free chocolate cake (and a ton of other GF goodies), it is her Gluten-Free Pie Dough that really blows me away—it's crispy and flaky and has that perfect pie mouthfeel. AND, unlike almost every other gluten-free pie dough I have made, you can actually pick hers up! As you can see from the list of ingredients below, it is not a simple flour substitution, but some very clever baking alchemy that allowed Courtney to accomplish this feat.

Yield: 1 double-crust pie

Ingredients

+ 240 grams (2 cups) Bob's Red Mill Gluten Free 1 to 1 Baking Flour
+ 30 grams (¼ cup) cornstarch
+ 1½ tablespoons caster sugar
+ 1 teaspoon salt
+ ½ teaspoon baking powder
+ 227 grams (16 tablespoons/1 cup) cold unsalted Kerrygold Pure Irish Butter (or other high-fat European-style butter)
+ 120 grams (½ cup) full-fat plain yogurt (ideally sheep yogurt, but you can also use strained Greek yogurt or sour cream)

Note: This dough will cook a little bit faster than a traditional piecrust (about 25 percent faster), so make sure to factor that into your baking plan.

1. About an hour before you want to make your dough, place a large metal mixing bowl in the fridge to chill it.

2. In the cold mixing bowl, whisk together the flour, cornstarch, sugar, salt, and baking powder.

3. Add the cold butter to the dry ingredients, cutting it into cubes.

Courtney Ford

4. Stir in the yogurt and "fluff up" the mixture until it looks like the photo on the opposite page.

5. Gently knead the dough until it comes together into tennis ball–size balls. It will initially seem like there is not enough moisture, but don't freak out! It will come together as you are gently kneading it.

6. Roll out your dough balls with a rolling pin into rectangular shapes sandwiched between two pieces of parchment paper. Fold the dough over twice like a sheet of paper going into an envelope, and then roll one more time. Repeat the fold, then wrap the rolled-out dough in plastic wrap and chill in the fridge for 1 hour, or up to overnight.

7. This dough will spread in the oven a fair bit because of the type of fats used, but you can minimize spreading by freezing your pie decoration before you bake it. If your pie goes into a hot oven directly from the freezer, it will have the best chance of retaining its form. Just remember to only do this with metal pie pans, never glass. Use the hashtag #GlutenFreeFord when you post your Pie Art using this recipe and follow Courtney on Instagram @courtneyfordhere!

I whipped up these crispy and delicious bunny pie pops while I was testing out this recipe, and they earned rave reviews from my family!

Liz Joy's Almond Cookie Pie Dough

Liz Joy, aka Elizabeth Murray, aka @InspiredToTaste, is probably no stranger to you if are a fan of Pie Art. Her stunning cookie crust and marshmallow fondant fantasy-themed pies have been wowing folks across the interwebs since 2018. And now she has graciously agreed to share with us her truly unique and delicious Almond Cookie Pie Dough recipe. It is so simple to make, yet results in a beautiful, crisp, lightly sweet cookie crust wthat you can then paint directly or complement with some of Liz's signature marshmallow fondant decorations. And bonus—it's suitable for people with low carb/low sugar and vegan diets!

Liz and I have been inspiring and challenging each other via our "Pie Art Collabs" for years, and every time we have one of our little pie-offs I think, "Damn! That's so good! I wish I made that!" Liz has always been super gracious about sharing her discoveries, disasters, and triumphs—she is a true kindred Pie Art spirit, and I am proud to call her my friend. On the opposite page is a photo of just one of the many gorgeous pies Liz has created with this recipe.

Yield: 1 top crust (you can double the recipe if you want a bottom crust too)

Ingredients

+ 135 grams (1½ cups) almond flour
+ 30 grams (¼ cup) arrowroot powder
+ 65 grams (⅓ cup) monk fruit sweetener (or equivalent sweetener)
+ 2 teaspoons ground cinnamon (or the flavoring of your choice)
+ 1 tablespoon vanilla bean paste
+ 3 tablespoons unsweetened applesauce

Liz Joy

1. Preheat the oven to 350°F (175°C; gas mark 4).

2. In a food proceswor, pulse together the almond flour, arrowroot powder, monk fruit sweetener, and cinnamon. If you don't have a food processor, simply mix the ingredients by hand.

3. Add the vanilla bean paste and applesauce to the food processor.

4. Process until the mixture comes together. The texture should be somewhat firm and hold together in a ball. If the dough is too dry, add a little more applesauce and pulse.

5. Roll out the dough approximately ⅛ inch (3 mm) thick, then press it into a pie pan. I stab the bottom with a fork a few times to avoid bubbling. Bake for 11 to 13 minutes, or until the edges start to deepen in color. Use the hashtag #InspiredToTastePieDough when you post your Pie Art using this recipe and check out InspiredToTaste.com and follow Liz on Instagram @InspiredToTaste!

One of Liz Joy's amazing pies

Kate McDermott's Half–Leaf Lard/ Half-Butter Pie Dough

Kate McDermott is the OG pie-oneer. She is a James Beard Award–nominated and best-selling author of three cookbooks, including the classic *Art of the Pie* and most recently *Pie Camp*. Kate has been passing on her prodigious pie knowledge for nearly twenty years, and I am honored to count her among my closest friends. I experienced my own personal "Pie Camp" a few years back when Kate accepted my invitation to come visit me in Vancouver, and I had the opportunity to test out her delicious, signature Half–Leaf Lard/Half-Butter Pie Dough recipe. On the opposite page is the pie we baked together.

Not only did Kate's recipe hold up beautifully with all my Pie Art techniques, but it was one of the best-tasting pies I ever had! I am so grateful Kate allowed me to share this recipe with you, and for her unfailing support and friendship over the years. Kate writes, teaches, and bakes with love, and it shows. Do yourself a favor and check out her classes (now virtual!) at artofthepie.com, or if you are ever in the Pacific Northwest, you can sign up for one of her in-person courses at Pie Cottage in Washington state. Just be warned, they sell out quick!

Yield: 1 double-crust pie

Ingredients

+ 363 grams (2½ cups) all-purpose flour
+ ½ teaspoon salt
+ 112 grams (8 tablespoons) unsalted butter, cut into tablespoon-size pieces
+ 112 grams (8 tablespoons) rendered leaf lard*, cut into tablespoon-size pieces
+ 118 grams (½ cup) ice water, plus 1 to 2 tablespoons as needed

If leaf lard isn't available at your local store, you can order it online. It is shelf-stable for up to 6 months.

Kate McDermott

1. Put all the ingredients except the ice water in a large mixing bowl.

2. With clean hands, quickly smoosh the mixture together, or use a pastry blender with an up-and-down motion, until the ingredients look like cracker crumbs with lumps the size of peas and almonds.

3. Sprinkle the ice water over the mixture and stir lightly with a fork. Squeeze a handful of dough to see if it holds together. Mix in more water as needed.

4. Divide the dough in half and make two chubby disks about 5 inches (12.5 cm) across. Wrap the disks separately in plastic wrap and chill for about an hour. Use the hashtag #ArtofthePieDough when you post your Pie Art using this recipe!

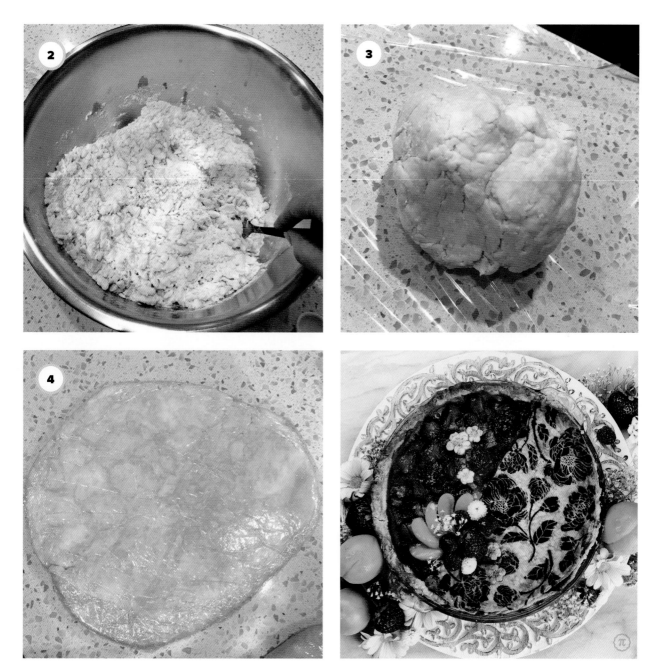

Kate's and my pie collaboration

Sugar-Free Apple Pie Filling

This was the very first pie filling I ever made, in response to my New Year's resolution to not eat any sugar for one year. I wanted to keep things simple because it was my first pie and not fiddle around with any thickeners or complicated chemical processes. I just prepared apples two different ways with spices, and when paired with a flaky sugar-free piecrust, it was absolutely delicious. Of course, my husband always dumped an extra heap of brown sugar onto his portions, but hey, it wasn't his resolution!

Yield: 1 standard-size pie

Ingredients

✦ 8 large apples, any variety

✦ 4 "crisp" apples (Granny Smith, Honeycrisp, Gala, Fuji, etc.)

✦ 1 tablespoon ground cinnamon

✦ 1 teaspoon ground nutmeg

✦ 80 grams (½ cup) brown sugar (optional)

1. Peel and dice the eight large apples into roughly 2-inch (5 cm) chunks.

2. Add enough water to a large saucepan to fill the bottom 1 inch (2.5 cm) high and bring to a boil. When the water is boiling, add the apple chunks and the cinnamon and nutmeg.

3. When the apple chunks are tender, use a potato masher to mash them up. (Don't worry about being thorough; it is fine to leave some chunks.) Continue boiling and stirring until the water has reduced by about half.

4. Remove the pan from the stove and strain the apples. You can keep the juice for something else, or just drink it!

5. Peel and cut the four "crisp" apples into ½-inch (1 cm) slices. Toss the slices in with the mashed apples and set the mixture aside to come to room temperature. At this point, you can mix in the brown sugar (if using) and any additional spices or flavoring you desire.

6. Once the filling has completely cooled, you can add it to your base pie to bake! Any leftover filling can be used to make pie pops or just eaten as is with a side of vanilla ice cream. Yum!

Canned Pie Filling Mod

Sometimes you don't have time to make a filling from scratch, but you just can't bring yourself to dump a couple of cans of pie filling into your base pie shell and call it a day. I get it! Canned filling is super convenient, but it does have a different mouthfeel and a lot more sugar than scratch-made recipes. So, what is a conscientious, time-crunched pie baker to do? Mod it!

That is, take a can of pie filling, dump it in a bowl, and add a cup of washed fresh fruit of the same variety and a few extra spices. Then transfer it to your base pie shell and bake as usual.

The added raw fruit will give the pie the texture and sophistication your guests expect from a scratch-made filling, while the thickeners in the canned-filling "goo" will ensure that it sets up perfectly with no extra work or ingredients required on your part! I'm particularly partial to making blueberry pies this way!

Yield: 1 standard-size pie

Ingredients

✦ 21-ounce (595 grams) blueberry pie filling of your choice

✦ 145 grams (1 cup) fresh blueberries

✦ 1 teaspoon lemon zest

✦ 1 teaspoon ground nutmeg

1. Pour the canned pie filling into a large mixing bowl.

2. Add the fresh blueberries, lemon zest, and ground nutmeg to the bowl and combine well.

3. Spoon the mixture into your base pie shell and bake as usual.

Banana Cream Cheese Icebox Pie Filling

Most of the pies in this book are paired with hot fillings meant to be served heated up. But sometimes it's nice to try something a little different (and, fair warning, a little more fattening!). This Banana Cream Cheese Filling is soooo creamy and delicious, and easy to prepare! Though you can pair it with traditional shortcrust, because the pie needs to be chilled before it is served, you are better off using a non-flaky crust, such as the Almond Cookie Pie Dough recipe on page 220 and the Sweet Pie Dough recipe on page 216, as they are especially fridge friendly.

Yield: 1 standard-size pie

Ingredients

✦ 118 grams (½ cup) whipping cream

✦ 1 teaspoon cream of tartar

✦ 8-ounce (227 grams) block cream cheese, softened

✦ 2 ripe bananas

✦ 100 grams (½ cup) caster sugar

1. With a stand mixer or hand mixer, whip the whipping cream with the cream of tartar. Set aside.

2. In a separate large mixing bowl, mash up the softened cream cheese, ripe bananas, and caster sugar until you have a smooth consistency.

3. Gently fold the whipped cream into the banana–cream cheese mixture with a rubber spatula.

4. If you will be filling tarts or PieKabob shells, spoon the mixture into a large piping bag; otherwise, spoon it directly into a cooled baked pie shell made with the dough of your choice.

5. Place the pie in the fridge to chill for at least 2 hours before decorating and serving.

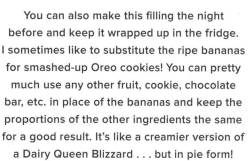

★ Jessica's Tip ★

You can also make this filling the night before and keep it wrapped up in the fridge. I sometimes like to substitute the ripe bananas for smashed-up Oreo cookies! You can pretty much use any other fruit, cookie, chocolate bar, etc. in place of the bananas and keep the proportions of the other ingredients the same for a good result. It's like a creamier version of a Dairy Queen Blizzard . . . but in pie form!

Preparing Your Base Pie

Now that you have your dough and filling recipes handy, you are ready to create the "base pie" that will support your lovely Pie Art decorations.

Icebox, Custard, and Curd Fillings

If your filling will be an icebox, custard, curd, or other particularly "wet" type of filling, you will need to prebake your crust either fully (blind baking) or partially (par-baking). Here's how:

1. Roll out your dough 3 inches (7.5 cm) larger than the pie pan all around and transfer it to the pie pan. Add the edge trim of your choice (unless it has an infinity edge), coat the bottom of the dough in a wash of your choice, dock (poke) the dough with a fork, and then pop it in the freezer for 10 minutes.

2. Line the chilled shell with a sheet of parchment paper and dump in some "pie weights." I use ceramic balls, but you can use rice, beans, a metal chain, or even sugar to weight your parchment down. Whatever you choose, just make sure it goes all the way up the sides of your pan so that the edges don't slump as it bakes. Place your pie pan on a baking sheet.

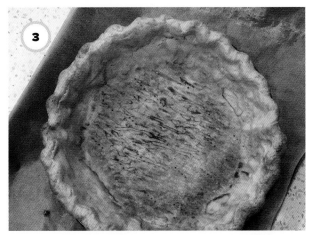

3. If **blind baking**, bake according to your recipe. If you don't have a recipe with specific blind-baking instructions, bake at 400°F (200°C; gas mark 6) for 15 minutes (350°F, or 175°C; gas mark 4, for cookie-style crusts). Remove the pie from the oven, carefully take out the parchment and pie weights, and bake for another 15 minutes, or until golden brown. If **par-baking**, take your pie out of the oven after 15 minutes and wait until the shell has cooled a bit to remove the weights.

4. After the pie base shell has cooled, you can add an extra layer of chocolate, jam, marzipan or anything else you think will enhance the flavor before you add the filling. (This step is optional.)

5. Once your filling has set, place your top decoration and serve!

Traditional Fillings

If your recipe doesn't call for your base pie shell to be blind-baked, then things are more straightforward. To prepare a base pie that will be baked with a traditional filling, follow these steps:

1. Roll out your dough 3 inches (7.5 cm) larger than the pie pan all around and transfer it to the pie pan. Add the edge trim of your choice (unless it has an infinity edge), coat the bottom of the dough in a wash of your choice, dock (poke) the dough with a fork, and then pop it in the freezer for 10 minutes.

2. Now add your *cooled* filling to the shell (never add warm filling to a pie shell unless you want a soggy bottom!).

3. If you have a crimped edge, protect it with some foil. Remove the foil for the last 10 or 15 minutes of the baking time. When baking a base pie with no top, some fillings can dry out a little; if this is a concern, loosely tent the top with foil.

4. Bake the base pie according to your recipe, or if your recipe doesn't specify a time and temperature, try 400°F (200°C; gas mark 6) for 50 minutes, or until the filling has been bubbling/boiling for 5 minutes. Don't judge by the doneness of the exposed trim! Uncovered trim can reach golden brown perfection long before the filling has set, and you will be left with a soggy bottom.

> ### ✷ Jessica's Tip ✷
>
> If you find that your bottoms are getting soggy anyway, try baking at 425°F (220°C; gas mark 7) for the first 15 minutes, and then reducing the heat to 350°F (175°C; gas mark 4) for another hour. Again, every oven is different, so what you really need to go by are those bubbles forming in the filling. Make sure you are baking your pie on a parchment-lined baking sheet and in a metal pan if you are worried about the doneness of the bottom!

5. The moment your base pie comes out of the oven, bubbling hot, have your top decoration and cake lifter at the ready. Carefully place the top decoration on top and lightly press down for 5 to 10 seconds so that the top and base fuse together. As the filling starts to set, the top and base pie will fuse together, and it will be as if your pie was baked as one piece.

Resources

My goal with this book is to provide the ultimate compendium of Pie Art techniques for bakers interested in taking their pie game to the next level. But for those of you who may not yet have a pie game to take to the next level, I want to make sure you still have access to a resource section that covers the basics: dough recipes, filling recipes, basic pie baking techniques like crimping, weaving, blind baking, and so on. Of course, I could fill a whole book with just these fundamentals (and many people before me have!), but then I would have a lot fewer pages to dedicate to all the fun new stuff!

In the interest of having our pie and eating it too, the happy medium I've hit upon is to provide a handful of the dough recipes I use most often here in the book and to host the rest of the resources for you online. This has the added benefit of ensuring that the links are evergreen, and that I can add to the sections as I make new discoveries and keep providing value to you for years to come!

All links and templates are available here:

https://www.piesareawesome.com/pages/resources

On this page, you will find links to resources on the following topics:

Templates
- All the templates used in the projects in this book, with usage instructions
- New and seasonal bonus templates for you!

Pie Art Community Resources
- Facebook pie community groups
- The best (and friendliest) Reddit communities for bakers
- An updated compendium of talented Pie Artists online for you to follow
- Highly regarded Pie Shops around the world
- Great pie baking courses and other relevant foodie courses online

Pie Science Stuff
- The science of pastry
- How to create flavor profiles
- How to create vibrant natural food colors
- How to check your oven for hot spots
- Recipe substitutions for diet restrictions
- The properties of pie pans
- Oven model comparisons

Recipes and Techniques

- Dough recipes I like

- Filling recipes I like

- How to blind-bake and par-bake piecrusts

- Pie edge-crimping styles

- Pie lattice-weaving techniques

- Creating chocolate decorations

Shopping Links

- All of the tools and ingredients used in this book

- Places to find some of the more esoteric Pie Art supplies, like food-safe freeze spray, 3-D cookie cutter printers, and Italian tart ring texture bands

- Other amazing pie and baking books that I think are worth checking out

- Honest product reviews

Business Resources

- Home-baker regulation links by region

- Setting up for farmers markets

- Tips on navigating social media as a baker

- General business setup

Cool Stuff and Inspiration

- Fine art collections

- Rights-free images

- Nature stuff

- Fashion stuff

- Historical pie facts

- Cool things that my creative friends are up to

My Social Media—Come Say Hi!

- Instagram: ThePieous

- Facebook: thepieous

- YouTube: PiesAreAwesome

- Twitter: ThePieous

- Reddit: ThePieous

- Newsletter and blog: piesareawesome.com

At these links, you'll find lots of new tutorials and fun open collabs, contests, baking prompts, product reviews, and pictures of my dog.

If there are other topics you would like me to add going forward, or if you have suggestions for businesses or individuals, I will consider adding them to the lists of Pie Artists and Pie Shops around the world. Just let me know at any of the links above!

The Pie Art Family

We're nearing the end of this book, and that means it's almost time for you to start whipping up some Pie Art of your own for your friends and family! But before we go, I want to introduce you to another family . . . the Pie Art Family.

Family? Really? Yes! The community of pastry artists online is an exceptionally supportive and kind one, filled with folks from all walks of life who embrace new members and openly share their knowledge and experience with newcomers. Consider this section your passport to this new world!

You are always welcome to lurk and scope out all the inspiring Pie Art on the down low, but when you are ready to dive in and start sharing your own creations, Instagram, Facebook, and Reddit are great places to start.

On **Instagram**, I hold monthly/seasonal Pie Art Challenges where I post a theme and hashtag, and folks play along by creating their own crusty creations on that theme . . . and yes, there are prizes! Check me out @thepieous for details on the next open collab.

On **Reddit**, you can join the r/Baking sub (Reddit.com/r/baking) and post photos of your Pie Art. "Sub" just means "sub community" within Reddit. Folks are fairly friendly in this particular sub, and if they really like your pie, it can "front page" (basically go viral) and be viewed by hundreds of thousands of people. But make sure you thoroughly read the community rules first. Unlike Instagram and Facebook, Reddit considers any self-promotion to be a big no-no.

Facebook has some delightful groups dedicated to pies, and increasingly Pie Art! Check out the groups "Pie Art" (run by yours truly), "Pie Baking Group" (run by Karen Scully), "Pie Nation" (run by Kate McDermott and Cathrine Gewertz), and "Passione Frolle" (run by Viviana Paiano). Lots of friendly people share recipes and advice, and a bit about their lives too!

Wherever you post your pies, use the hashtag at the bottom of each project along with #PiesAreAwesomeTheBook and I'll be able to find you and come check out your work. I can't wait to see your creations!

If you're looking for a little more inspiration in the Pie Art department, a number of my buddies have graciously given me permission to share with you some of my favorite artsy pies out there today. My first thought upon looking at each of these pies was "Daymn! I wish I had made that!" And whenever I have that reaction to something, I know that I have to reach out to the artist and make friends with them immediately! I am delighted to say that every one of them turned out to be a super-awesome, friendly person who didn't mind my weird fan-girling over their work. Check out their accounts! They're all great about responding to questions and comments about their work, and I hope you find their bakes as inspiring as I do.

While I'm crazy about these nine pie designs, there are about a hundred gazillion more that I also love, and I want to share them all with you! But my editor told me that I couldn't add an extra seventy-two pages for that, so I'll have to content myself with just a list of the Pie Artists' Instagram accounts (see page 232). If you like what you see, give 'em a follow! And I hope by my next book, I'll be able to add your name to the list too . . .

Instagram: @inspiredtotaste
Real name: Liz Joy
(Check out her Almond Cookie Pie
Dough recipe on page 220!)

Instagram: @arlodesigns
Real name: Arlene Lott

Instagram: @oldfashionedbaker
Real name: Александр (Sacha)
Кудрявцев

Instagram: @mksplendidcake
Real name: Marina Kojukhova

Instagram: @luxeandthelady
Real name: Jessica Lucius

Instagram: @instamerrill.foodart
Real name: Merrill Walker

Instagram: @wu.ciesielska
Real name: Weronika Ciesielska

Instagram: @stratiatelier
Real name: Rita Strati

Instagram: @loriastern
Real name: Loria Stern

Jessica's "Must-Follow" List

- chefcalum
- juliejones_uk
- karinpfeiffboschek
- batterednbaked
- lokokitchen
- stratiatelier
- acarriedaffairdesigns
- aphrahannahbakes
- batchpleasecookies
- beeandthebaker
- bels_pies
- blackbirdartisanpieco
- bonbonbaked
- broadwaybaking
- cakeit.till.you.makeit
- cakesbykristi
- callumasplen
- chandrasosweet
- chouxdefoudre
- christiemakesthings
- coderxbaker

- devoneybakes
- fortyninefigs
- ghouliachilds
- gryffinn.dor
- hannahspiesandthings
- happiness.is.apieceofcake
- happy.go.lucky.little.me
- jennifer.d.love
- jojoromancer
- kathryn_lb
- katie_medendorp
- kfreidt
- la.reyna.patisserie
- laroxy72
- lildamecake
- lisamakespie
- loriastern
- luciabusinelli
- mariesaba
- miscottodolci
- momdaysofsummer

- nancybakerfoodartist
- onceuponapiebakery
- paianoviviana
- pieladybooks
- pie_goddess
- pribakes
- rosensteintimea
- sayitwithsweetsbyjools
- screamandsugarpies
- scully.karen
- suburban_pie
- sugaryums
- tanyaskitchen
- tarts_and_fairytales
- thecraftingfoodie
- thecrumbcrush
- the_fairy_bakester
- torte_a_colori
- _aisforapplepie
- _ghoul_mom

There are literally hundreds more that I could list, but I know you'll for sure find some kindred pie spirits in this list!

Oh, and before I move on, I also wanted to give a shout-out to four special Pie Artists who, while they don't do "figurative" Pie Art, are undoubtedly in the must-follow category for their pure mastery of pastry:

- Kate McDermott: @katemcdermott
- Erin Jeanne McDowell: @emcdowell
- Chris Taylor & Paul Arguin: @floursugarbutter

They are truly pie whisperers. I adore their flavorful and unique recipes and I know you will too!

Now what are you waiting for? Come make some new Pie Art friends!

Index

A

adhesives, edible, 28
Advanced projects
  La Catrina Pie, 144–149
  Paris Skyline Pie, 124–129
  Piescraper, 199–205
  Sugar Plum Fairy Pie Doll, 169–175
all-butter dough
  all-butter shortcrust, 18–19
  Chibi Pumpkin Pie, 136–139
  Flying Unicorn Pie, 186–189
  Gelt Pie, 164–167
  Goofy Turkey Pie, 151–153
  Harvest Tree Pie, 154–157
  introduction to, 18–19
  Leprechaun Hat Pie, 92–97
  Mama and Baby Bear Pies, 194–197
  Mandala Pie, 131–135
  Monster Mouth Pie, 141–143
  Paris Skyline Pie, 124–129
  pâte brisée, 19
  patê sablée, 21
  puff pastry, 20
  Quilt Pie, 111–115
  rough puff, 20
  Shirt and Tie Pie, 116–119
  Stars and Stripes Pie, 121–123
  Tic-Tac-Toe Pie, 84–87
all-lard shortcrust
  Folk Art Bee Pie, 104–109
  Gelt Pie, 164–167
  Goofy Turkey Pie, 151–153
  Harvest Tree Pie, 154–157
  introduction to, 19
  Lantern Festival Pie, 81–83
  Leprechaun Hat Pie, 92–97
  Mama and Baby Bear Pies, 194–197
  Mandala Pie, 131–135
  Monster Mouth Pie, 141–143
  Paris Skyline Pie, 124–129
  Pi Pie, 89–91
  Quilt Pie, 111–115
  Santa Claus Pie, 176–181
  Shirt and Tie Pie, 116–119
  Stars and Stripes Pie, 121–123
  Tic-Tac-Toe Pie, 84–87
all-shortening shortcrust
  Bunny Pie, 99–103
  Clock Pie, 183–185
  Folk Art Bee Pie, 104–109

Gelt Pie, 164–167
Goofy Turkey Pie, 151–153
Harvest Tree Pie, 154–157
introduction to, 19
La Catrina Pie, 144–149
Lantern Festival Pie, 81–83
Leprechaun Hat Pie, 92–97
Mama and Baby Bear Pies, 194–197
Mandala Pie, 131–135
Monster Mouth Pie, 141–143
Paris Skyline Pie, 124–129
Pi Pie, 89–91
Quilt Pie, 111–115
Santa Claus Pie, 176–181
Shirt and Tie Pie, 116–119
Stars and Stripes Pie, 121–123
Sugar Plum Fairy Pie Doll, 169–175
  Tic-Tac-Toe Pie, 84–87
  Almond Cookie Pie Dough, 220–221
apples
  Bunny Pie, 99–103
  Flying Unicorn Pie, 186–189
  Harvest Tree Pie, 154–157
  Leprechaun Hat Pie, 92–97
  Quilt Pie, 111–115
  Stars and Stripes Pie, 121–123
  Sugar-Free Apple Pie Filling, 224
Arguin, Paul, 232
assembly
  best practices, 63–64
  domed pies, 64
  dough thickness, 65
  freeze spray, 65
  hot pastry, 65
  melt options, 65
  moisture control, 65

B

Banana Cream Cheese Icebox Pie Filling
  Folk Art Bee Pie, 104–109
  PieKabobs, 191–193
  recipe, 225
  base pie preparation, 226–227
Beginner projects
  Chibi Pumpkin Pie, 136–139
  Flying Unicorn Pie, 186–189
  Gelt Pie, 164–167
  Goofy Turkey Pie, 151–153
  Harvest Tree Pie, 154–157

Mama and Baby Bear Pies, 194–197
Monster Mouth Pie, 141–143
PieKabobs, 191–193
Pi Pie, 89–91
Quilt Pie, 111–115
Shirt and Tie Pie, 116–119
Snowman Pie, 159–163
Tic-Tac-Toe Pie, 84–87
blackberries
Folk Art Bee Pie, 104–109
Paris Skyline Pie, 124–129
blueberries
Canned Pie Filling Mod, 224
Folk Art Bee Pie, 104–109
Paris Skyline Pie, 124–129
Stars and Stripes Pie, 121–123
Boschek, Karin Pfeiff, 31

C

celebrations. See also holidays.
Baby Shower, 194–197, 209
Birthday, 186–189, 191–193, 209
Wedding, 199–205, 209
cherries
PieKabobs, 191–193
Stars and Stripes Pie, 121–123
chess: Goofy Turkey Pie, 151–153
Ciesielska, Weronika, 231
color
brushes, 46–47
edible emulsifiers, 44–45
edible powders, 59
feathering, 72
natural food colors, 73
post-baked dough, 46
pre-baked dough, 45–46
pre-mixed dough, 46
selection of, 44
troubleshooting, 47
vanilla wash, 45
cookie-style dough
Almond Cookie Pie Dough, 220–221
Bunny Pie, 99–103
Chibi Pumpkin Pie, 136–139
Clock Pie, 183–185
Flying Unicorn Pie, 186–189
Folk Art Bee Pie, 104–109
Gelt Pie, 164–167
Goofy Turkey Pie, 151–153
Harvest Tree Pie, 154–157
La Catrina Pie, 144–149
Lantern Festival Pie, 81–83
Leprechaun Hat Pie, 92–97
Mama and Baby Bear Pies, 194–197
Mandala Pie, 131–135

Monster Mouth Pie, 141–143
Paris Skyline Pie, 124–129
pasta frolla/pâte sucrée, 20
PieKabobs, 191–193
Pi Pie, 89–91
Piescraper, 199–205
Quilt Pie, 111–115
Sweet Pie Dough, 216–217
Santa Claus Pie, 176–181
Shirt and Tie Pie, 116–119
Snowman Pie, 159–163
Stars and Stripes Pie, 121–123
Sugar Plum Fairy Pie Doll, 169–175
Tic-Tac-Toe Pie, 84–87
Corneo, Elisabetta, 31
Courtney Ford's Gluten-Free Pie Dough, 218–219
crimped-edge pies
Bunny Pie, 99–103
Chibi Pumpkin Pie, 136–139
Flying Unicorn Pie, 186–189
Folk Art Bee Pie, 104–109
Gelt Pie, 164–167
Goofy Turkey Pie, 151–153
Harvest Tree Pie, 154–157
introduction to, 60–61
Lantern Festival Pie, 81–83
Mandala Pie, 131–135
Quilt Pie, 111–115
Stars and Stripes Pie, 121–123
Tic-Tac-Toe Pie, 84–87

D

display
complementary decor, 70
dessert stands, 69
trim rings, 69–70
dough. See also specific types.
bake times, 22–24
chilling, 39, 41–42
coloring, 44–47
comparison chart, 18
cut direction, 42
cutters, 52
cutting tricks, 41–43
double-dough method, 67
fluffy edges, 43
found objects, 53
handling technique, 39–40
hot-water crust, 19–20
household heat and, 74
introduction to, 17
method of creation, 17–18
moisture barriers, 26
molds, 54–56
plunger cutters, 53

post-baked color, 46
pre-bake colors, 45–46
precision blades and, 41
pre-mixed colors, 46
pressing to cut, 42–43
rolling technique, 37–39
sculpting, 50–51
stainless-steel shortcut, 43
store-bought dough, 21
structural testing, 24
test chart, 23
testing, 22–24
thickness, 65, 72
troubleshooting, 71–72
workspace for, 35–36

E

edible adhesives, 28
egg whites, pasteurized, 28

F

fillings
  Banana Cream Cheese Icebox Pie Filling, 225
  base pie preparation, 226–227
  Canned Pie Filling Mod, 224
  introduction to, 25–26
  Sugar-Free Apple Pie Filling, 224
Ford, Courtney, 20, 218
Franklin, Calum, 31

G

garnishes, 27–28
glazes, 27
gluten-free dough
  introduction to, 20
  recipe, 218–219
  Goldman, Duff, 8–9

H

half-butter/half-lard shortcrust
  Folk Art Bee Pie, 104–109
  Gelt Pie, 164–167
  Goofy Turkey Pie, 151–153
  half–leaf lard/half-butter dough, 222–223
  Harvest Tree Pie, 154–157
  introduction to, 19
  Leprechaun Hat Pie, 92–97
  Mama and Baby Bear Pies, 194–197
  Mandala Pie, 131–135
  Monster Mouth Pie, 141–143
  Paris Skyline Pie, 124–129
  Pi Pie, 89–91
  Quilt Pie, 111–115
  Santa Claus Pie, 176–181

  Shirt and Tie Pie, 116–119
  Tic-Tac-Toe Pie, 84–87
half-butter/half-shortening shortcrust
  Folk Art Bee Pie, 104–109
  Gelt Pie, 164–167
  Goofy Turkey Pie, 151–153
  Harvest Tree Pie, 154–157
  introduction to, 19
  Leprechaun Hat Pie, 92–97
  Mama and Baby Bear Pies, 194–197
  Mandala Pie, 131–135
  Monster Mouth Pie, 141–143
  Paris Skyline Pie, 124–129
  Pi Pie, 89–91
  Quilt Pie, 111–115
  recipe, 212–213
  Santa Claus Pie, 176–181
  Shirt and Tie Pie, 116–119
  Tic-Tac-Toe Pie, 84–87
Half–Leaf Lard/Half-Butter Pie Dough, 222–223
holidays. See also celebrations.
  Bastille Day, 124–129, 207
  Christmas, 169–175, 176–181, 208, 209
  Day of the Dead, 144–149, 208
  Diwali, 131–135, 207
  Earth Day, 104–109, 206
  Easter, 99–103, 206
  Father's Day, 116–119, 207
  Fourth of July, 121–123, 207
  Halloween, 136–139, 141–143, 207, 208
  Hanukkah, 164–167, 208
  Lunar New Year, 81–83, 206
  Mother's Day, 111–115
  New Year's Eve, 183–185, 209
  Pi Day, 89–91, 206
  St. Patrick's Day, 92–97, 206
  Thanksgiving, 151–153, 154–157, 208
  Valentine's Day, 84–87, 206
  Winter Holidays, 159–163, 208
hot-water crust, 19–20

I

infinity-edge pies
  Clock Pie, 183–185
  introduction to, 60
  La Catrina Pie, 144–149
  Leprechaun Hat Pie, 92–97
  Mama and Baby Bear Pies, 194–197
  Monster Mouth Pie, 141–143
  Paris Skyline Pie, 124–129
  Pi Pie, 89–91
  Santa Claus Pie, 176–181
  Shirt and Tie Pie, 116–119
  Snowman Pie, 159–163
Intermediate projects

Bunny Pie, 99–103
Clock Pie, 183–185
Folk Art Bee Pie, 104–109
Lantern Festival Pie, 81–83
Leprechaun Hat Pie, 92–97
Mandala Pie, 131–135
Santa Claus Pie, 176–181
Stars and Stripes Pie, 121–123

J

Jones, Julie, 31
Joy, Liz, 20, 31, 220, 221, 231

K

Kate McDermott's Half–Leaf Lard/Half-Butter Pie Dough, 222–223
Kojukhova, Marina, 231
Ko, Lauren, 31

L

Liz Joy's Almond Cookie Pie Dough, 220–221
Lott, Arlene, 231
Lucius, Jessica, 231

M

McDermott, Kate, 19, 222, 230, 232
McDowell, Erin Jeanne, 232
meringues
    Santa Claus Pie, 176–181
    Snowman Pie, 159–163
    Sugar Plum Fairy Pie Doll, 169–175
mincemeat: Paris Skyline Pie, 124–129
modding ideas
    Bunny Pie, 103
    Chibi Pumpkin Pie, 139
    Clock Pie, 185
    Flying Unicorn Pie, 189
    Folk Art Bee Pie, 109
    Gelt Pie, 167
    Goofy Turkey Pie, 153
    Harvest Tree Pie, 157
    La Catrina Pie, 149
    Lantern Festival Pie, 83
    Leprechaun Hat Pie, 97
    Mama and Baby Boar Pies, 107
    Mandala Pie, 135
    Monster Mouth Pie, 143
    Paris Skyline Pie, 129
    PieKabobs, 192
    Piescraper, 204
    Pi Pie, 91
    Quilt Pie, 115
    Santa Claus Pie, 181
    Shirt and Tie Pie, 119

Snowman Pie, 163
Stars and Stripes Pie, 123
Sugar Plum Fairy Pie Doll, 174
Tic-Tac-Toe Pie, 87
moisture barriers, 26
Murray, Elizabeth. See Joy, Liz.

P

pasta frolla/pâte sucrée, 20
pasteurized egg whites, 28
pâte brisée, 19
patê sablée, 21
piescrapers
    armatures, 68
    double-dough method, 67
    Piescraper project, 199–205
    standees, 66–67
    tall pie pans, 67
planning
    design metrics, 75–76
    visual inspiration, 76–77
    workspace and, 36
puff pastry, 20
pumpkins
    Chibi Pumpkin Pie, 136–139
    Goofy Turkey Pie, 151–153

R

raspberries: Gelt Pie, 164–167
rough puff, 20

S

shortcrust
    all-butter shortcrust, 18–19
    all-lard shortcrust, 19
    all-shortening shortcrust, 19
    half-butter/half-lard shortcrust, 19, 222–223
    half-butter/half-shortening shortcrust, 19, 212–213
stencils
    best practices, 57–59
    Quilt Pie, 111–115
Stern, Loria, 231
store-bought dough, 21
Strati, Rita, 31, 231
supplies
    armatures, 68
    basic supplies, 34
    border molds, 56
    brushes, 16–17
    complementary decor, 70
    cutters, 52
    decorating ingredients, 34
    dessert stands, 69
    food-safe plastics, 33

found objects, 53
freeze spray, 65
impression mats, 56
molds, 54–56
must-have supplies, 32
next-level supplies, 33
nice-to-have supplies, 33
parchment paper, 35, 72, 73
plunger cutters, 53
precision blades, 41
standees, 66–67
tall pie pans, 67
trim rings, 69–70
Sweet Pie Dough
    PieKabobs, 191–193
    Piescraper, 199–205
    recipe, 216–217
    Snowman Pie, 159–163
    Sugar Plum Fairy Pie Doll, 169–175
sweet potato: Goofy Turkey Pie, 151–153

T

Taylor, Chris, 232
templates
    best practices, 49
    Bunny Pies, 206
    Chibi Pumpkin Pie, 207
    Clock Pie, 209
    cutting, 48–49
    Flying Unicorn Pie, 209
    Folk Art Bee Pie, 206
    Gelt Pie, 208
    Goofy Turkey Pie, 208
    Harvest Tree Pie, 208
    introduction to, 48–49
    La Catrina Pie, 208
    Lantern Festival Pie, 206
    Leprechaun Hat Pie, 206
    Mama and Baby Bear Pies, 209
    Mandala Pie, 207
    Monster Mouth Pie, 208
    Paris Skyline Pie, 207
    Piescraper, 209
    Pi Pie, 206
    printing, 48
    Santa Claus Pie, 209
    Shirt and Tie Pie, 207
    Snowman Pie, 208
    Stars and Stripes Pie, 207
    Sugar Plum Fairy Pie Doll, 208
    Tic-Tac-Toe Pie, 206
trends, 29–31
trim designs
    appliqués, 61–62
    braids, 61
    crimped edge, 60–61
    infinity edge, 60, 62
    molded trim, 61
    twists, 61
troubleshooting
    air bubbles, 72
    burned decorations, 73
    color, 47
    color feathering, 72
    complete and total disaster, 74
    crust damage, 73
    dough, 71–72
    falling decorations, 73
    fluffy edges, 43
    kitchen fires, 73
    molds, 55–56
    parfait solution, 74
    result variations, 74
    soggy crust, 73

V

vanilla wash, 45
Vegan Pie Dough, 214–215

W

Walker, Merrill, 231
washes, 27
workspace
    clean space, 36
    dough-prep area, 35–36
    environmental adjustments, 36
    introduction to, 35
    main dough stage, 35
    parchment paper, 35
    planning and, 36
    tool storage, 36
    wet supplies, 36

SYMBOLS

Кудрявцев, Александр (Sacha), 231

Acknowledgments

My acknowledgements are long. OK, really long. This is true.

But what's also true is that each and every person listed here has played an integral part in making this book a reality. Every person listed here has helped me either professionally, financially, philosophically, emotionally, or mentally by giving me what I needed most, when I needed it most, to keep moving forward with my wacky pie dreams! Sometimes this was accomplished by providing advice on how not to blow up a New York client's studios with edible napalm (thanks, Doug!) or to tell me that my Chinese symbols were backward (thanks, Pen!). Sometimes it was helping me pay for the equipment I needed to take my work to the next level (looking at you, Jenny and Greg!), and other times it was as simple as making me feel like what I was doing was worthwhile with a kind word perfectly phrased and timed just right.

My heartfelt thanks to each and every one of you—I hope you enjoy the book that your support has helped create, and I hope I can continue to create work that will put a smile on your lovely faces for many years to come!

First, to my immediate family and bestest friends, who have literally kept me alive this past year: Nis Bojin, Cillian Clark-Bojin, Bernie Clark, Violette Clark, Ryan Clark, Kathryn Skyes, Claudine and Reinhard Boerner (aka Nanny and Opa), Sebastien de Castell, and Christina de Castell.

Next, to the first people who believed in me and my business, and those who helped me level up big time: Jennifer Quano, Greg Zeschuk, Kate Kenny, Matt Toner, and Duff Goldman.

To the folks at The Quarto Group for saying, "Hey, wanna do a book?" and then helping me do just that: Rage Kindelsperger, Erin Canning, Laura Drew, Todd Conly, and the editorial, design, and sales teams!

To the supportive clients, partners, TV bookers, and journalists who have been extra kind to me:

FOOD Network, Smuckers Canada, Country Music Television, The Royal Canadian Mint, the *Today* show, *Food & Wine Magazine*, Bored Panda, Wilton, and Ripley's Believe It or Not!

To the folks who have taught me and helped me refine my pie-deas, recipes, photos, business plans, and to become a better baker and artist: My best pie friend, Kate McDermott, Doug Stephen, Lindsey Mann, Ksenia Penkina, Stewart Ward, Courtney Ford and Brandon Routh (and L!), Delphine Doreau, and Elisabeth "Liz Joy" Murray.

To my intrepid recipe testers: lead recipe tester Karen Scully and additional recipe testers Viviana Paiano, Christina de Castell, Annette Arndt, Siobhan Louise O'Keefe, Shanna Pederson, April Green, and Sandra Rojas-Gonzalez.

To my good-humored cultural consultants: Pen-hsuan Hsing, Amanda Wong, Jeet Samra, and Sandra Rojas-Gonzalaz.

And if I've looked marginally presentable, it's because of these lovely people: Ami K at Line Spa and Polish (@nail_sbyami @linespaandpolish), Dr. Christopher Pavlou at Skin Technique (@skintechnique), and Emily Merey at Citrus Hair Salon (@citrushairsalon).

To the absolute village of awesome people who've always had my back when the internet trolls troll, who've helped spread the word for my Kickstarter and other kooky projects, and who keep me motivated with words of encouragement every day: Dr. James Clark (aka Uncle Jimmy), Ali de Levie, Brandon Heagle, Cathi Anderson, Debbie Nordbruget, Graham Venn, Kari Winfield, Kerry Heagle, Leslie Brown, Linda Heagle, Lisa Anderson, Marc Anderson, Martine de Levie, Mat Heagle, Maureen and Eric Sykes, Maureen Nordbruget, Mike Clark, Nathalie Keiller, Rene Heagle, Sam and Toby

Clark, Sara Baird, Shana Heagle, Tom and Pernille Bojin, Wendy Bojin-Liston, Aimee Falkenberg, Alicia Peloquin White, Alison Fox, Alistair MacLeod, Amy Bee, Amy Nazarewich, Angela Melgaard Tomizu, Anne Thériault, Annette Arndt, April Green, Ariel Chao, Ash Turner, Barbara Wallace, Barrie Tullett, Beata Kacy, Ben Stenbeck, Brenda Dedrick, Brett Forsyth, Caro Chibau, Carole Malecot-Quaite, Chris Bjerrisgaard, Christine Lim-Labossiere, Danika Dinsmore, Dannie Zhao, Dan Toews, Dave Warfield, David Geertz, David Luce, Debra Frances Plant-Humphries, Devon Larson-Reis, Diana Batts, Eleanore Nuttall, Erica-Dawn Egan, Eric Bjorndal, Erin Catania-Hobbis, Ethan Graham Peacock, Gagan Diesh, Gay McCoan, George Georgeadis, Georg Zoeller, Gina Szymczak Hall, Grant Olsen, Ingrid Frauenstein, Jaala Leis Wanless, Jack Derong, Jai Djwa, Jake Birkett, James Devon, James Ritzman, Jeff Morris, Jenaya Ciavarro, Jennica Harper, Jennifer Siddle, Jericca Cleland, Jim Valentino, Johnathon Von Strebly, John Langrish, Johnna Goldman, Jules Seaman, Justin Ramsden, Karen Lam, Kathy Healy Madison, Kat Montagu, Kat Zeller, Kenton Loewen, Lawrence Gowan, Len Lendvoy, Lisa Howatt Hamel, Lousie Lee, Lucie (Bakes) Radcliffe, Ludi Lin, Lynette Killam, Malcom Thomas-Gustave, Marissa Anne Wright, Mary-Anne Crevier, Maxine Barton Finch, Maya Saxell, Megan Humphrey, Mikela Jay, Mike Lee, Morgan Jeske, Patsy Tomkins, Patti Larsen, Paula Simson, R. Morgan Slade, Radhika Mathur Mellin, Reinhard Pekarek, Renee Laprise, Rob Kim, Robyn Wiener, Ruth Atherley, Sacha Szymczak, Sarah Elizabeth, Scott Mignola, Sean Dillon, Sergio Toporek, Shaundra Curtis, Shae Hobbis, Sidika Larbes, Siobhan Louise O'Keefe, Stanislava Schmakin, Stephen Hui, Stephen Webster, Sue Ciavarro, Susan Keeping, Susan Manning, Susan Nation, Terry Lanthier, Tom Belding, Torrey Huxley, Trevor Holness, Trilby Jeeves, Tyler Sigman, Victoria Pearson, Wendy D, Wil Arndt, Wincy Aquino Ong, The fine folks at BrickCan and VLUG, Jenell Parsons and The Pie Hole in Vancouver (best mini pies!), The Gourmet Warehouse in Vancouver (best baking supplies!), and the florists at the Bloomerie in Vancouver (best styling of flowers!). Lastly, a huge thank you to every person listed in the Pie Art Family section on page 230! You and your marvelous creativity make it all worthwhile.

And to those people I have accidentally left off the list—doh! My bad, but thanks to you too. I owe you a pie!

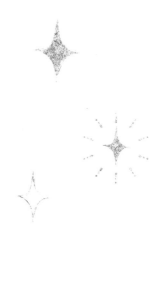

About Jessica

Hello! You've made it all the way to the end of *Pies Are Awesome* . . . I hope you liked it! And I really hope I'll get to see some of your own Pie Art creations soon. I would love to hear what you thought of the book in general, so if you get a chance, please share your review on Goodreads or Amazon. All feedback is welcome! It's always nerve-racking putting something you create out into the world, but I wouldn't have it any other way.

Jessica Leigh Clark-Bojin, Cillian Clark-Bojin, and Nis Bojin

Jessica's dog, Witty

Whenever I'm asked to introduce myself "in a sentence" at a networking event or business-type situation, I lead with "My name is Jessica. I like to make things and make things happen," which is all very concise, but it doesn't really capture the complete picture. It's true. I am very passionate about making things, and I have a habit of excitedly roping in the people around me to join in on my creative schemes . . . but what are those things I like to make?

So many things!

In my time on this planet so far, I've studied physics, played guitar in a garage punk band, drawn and edited comics, produced indie films, led a business department at Vancouver Film School, taught stage fighting and fencing, created children's art camps and birthday parties, given talks at San Diego Comic Con, hosted shoebox-diorama competitions for grown-ups, designed vinyl art toys . . . <big breath> . . . and now I bake pies! All I know is that I love to learn new things, and I love to teach—and teaching and sharing what I know is my favorite way to learn!

I also absolutely adore meeting new creative people, and if our paths cross and we become friends, you can bet at some point an invitation will be extended to a sci-fi-themed tea party, a miniature D&D figure painting session, or to come over and listen to Pink Floyd while reading comic books and playing with LEGO (card-carrying AFoL right here!).

But more than anything, I love spending time with family, my awesome nerdy family, who have always been there for me, encouraging and supporting my decades of wacky adventures!

If you'd like to learn more about my career as a Pie Artist, or have any questions, come check out piesareawesome.com.

Jessica's LEGO sigfig